Making ADD Work

Making A·D·D Work

On-the-Job Strategies for Coping with Attention Deficit Disorder

Blythe Grossberg, Psy.D.

A Perigee Book

THE BERKLEY PUBLISHING GROUP
Published by the Penguin Group
Penguin Group (USA) Inc.
375 Hudson Street, New York, New York 10014, USA
Penguin Group (Canada), 10 Alcorn Avenue, Toronto, Ontario M4V 3B2, Canada
(a division of Pearson Penguin Canada Inc.)
Penguin Books Ltd., 80 Strand, London WC2R 0RL, England
Penguin Group Ireland, 25 St. Stephen's Green, Dublin 2, Ireland (a division of Penguin Books Ltd.)
Penguin Group (Australia), 250 Camberwell Road, Camberwell, Victoria 3124, Australia
(a division of Pearson Australia Group Pty. Ltd.)
Penguin Books India Pvt. Ltd., 11 Community Centre, Panchsheel Park, New Delhi–110 017, India
Penguin Books (NZ), cnr. Airborne and Rosedale Roads, Albany, Auckland 1310, New Zealand
(a division of Pearson New Zealand Ltd.)
Penguin Books (South Africa) (Pty.) Ltd., 24 Sturdee Avenue, Rosebank, Johannesburg 2196,
South Africa
Penguin Books Ltd., Registered Offices: 80 Strand, London WC2R 0RL, England

Copyright © 2005 by Blythe Grossberg
Text design by Kristin del Rosario
Cover design by Mark S. Pardini and Petra Andersson-Pardini

PRINTING HISTORY
Perigee trade paperback edition / September 2005

PERIGEE is a registered trademark of Penguin Group (USA) Inc.
The "P" design is a trademark belonging to Penguin Group (USA) Inc.

Library of Congress Cataloging-in-Publicaion Data

Grossberg, Blythe N.
    Making ADD work : practical strategies for maximizing your talents and getting ahead / by Blythe N. Grossberg.
        p. cm.
    Includes bibliographical references and index.
    ISBN 0-399-53199-8
    1. Attention-deficit disorder in adults. 2. Attention-deficit hyperactivity disorder. I. Title.

RC394.A85G76 2005
616.85'89–dc22

                                                            2005043123

PRINTED IN THE UNITED STATES OF AMERICA

10 9 8 7 6 5 4 3 2 1

Acknowledgments

First and foremost, I'd like to thank the subjects of this book, who trusted me to tell their stories. I spent many enjoyable hours finding out about their rich, wonderful lives, and this book is my gift to them in the hope that they may benefit from the wisdom of other ADD adults. It was great fun to be let into their lives for a short time. Scott Eyre spoke to me from spring training with the San Francisco Giants, and I thank him for providing insight into the fascinating world of professional baseball. Jennifer Stewart spoke to me about her life as Lady Liberty and her inspiring career. The other participants remain nameless, but the time they gave me provided this book with its inspiration.

The people at Perigee were unfailingly warm and encouraging. My editor, Marian Lizzi, is unequaled in talent, vision, and sweetness. Her assistant, Laurie Cedilnik, was always helpful and efficient, and copyeditor Christy Wagner corrected my errors with a neat, observant hand. Thanks to the publisher, John Duff, and to former editor Sheila Curry-Oakes for believing in the book and taking this project on.

Thanks to Bryan Baldwin and Gareth Edmondson-Jones at JetBlue Airways for getting CEO David Neeleman's preface off the ground, and to Mr. Neeleman and Terry Matlen, M.S.W., A.C.S.W., for taking time out of their busy lives to write introductions that shared their personal experiences with ADD.

My original agent, Jessica Papin at Dystel & Goderich Literary Management, is the tops, and I couldn't wish for a better person to shepherd the book through publication than Michael Bourret, who is the most diligent, smart, and patient agent I could imagine.

Many people have helped me integrate my interests in writing and psychology, including my giving, brilliant professors at Rutgers: Clay and Charleen Alderfer, Cary Cherniss, Ruth Orenstein, Kenneth Schneider, Karen Skean, Christine Truhe, and others. Rachel Kahan encouraged me to keep writing through many, many dispiriting rejections. Patty Laufer and Judith Levy Cohen provided guidance and mentorship in my work.

My parents, Jill and Bernard Grossberg, always gave me notebooks for my birthdays and told me to keep writing; my grandparents, Evelyn and David Grossberg, gave me the "writing genes"; and my twin brother, Josh, kept me company while reading. My husband, John Dorfman, made it all worthwhile with his love and companionship.

Contents

Preface

by David Neeleman, CEO of JetBlue Airways

In my entrepreneurial career, during which I founded the most successful start-up airline in aviation history, I've always had the gut feeling that having ADD has worked to my great advantage. That was true even before I knew I had ADD—I just knew I didn't quite think the same as a lot of other people. In fact, looking back over my career, I believe that having ADD has set me apart from the pack and allowed me to see possibilities and frontiers of aviation that weren't visible to my competitors.

My elementary-school teachers would probably be surprised to hear me say this. School wasn't always suited to my tastes and talents as a kid. When I was supposed to be doing long division or tackling a spelling test, my mind tended to wander. It usually flew right out the window—and into the wild blue yonder, where I would imagine jets cruising past the sound barrier.

Once I left school, however, I found that my unique ways of thinking and being—ways that hadn't always led me to overwhelming success in school—started to pay off. I wasn't afraid to seize the opportunities that presented themselves to me, just as I wasn't afraid to get on any plane, anytime, anywhere.

My career has always involved seeing beyond the obvious and taking the next step. I founded two other discount airlines that I later sold, invented ticketless travel, and started a real "passenger revolution" at JetBlue Airways that finally gave people the opportunity to fly safely, comfortably, and inexpensively. Before I started JetBlue, it was downright obvious to me that there was room for an airline with friendly staff who actually made flying fun—an idea that hadn't yet really occurred to anyone else. And the idea that this airline could take off from busy JFK Airport in New York City was a double challenge to conventional wisdom, and one that we proved right.

My restless nature has reaped big rewards for our dedicated crewmembers and our customers. While my tendency to fidget used to get me detention in school, it now means that I'm always up in the air, flying and finding out more about what my customers want and need. Spontaneity, creativity, restlessness—not qualities I was rewarded for in school, but talents that come partly from having ADD and that provide special advantages in the business world.

Though I've always known that these qualities can be advantageous for entrepreneurs and other people in the work world, I've rarely seen the positive side of adult ADD mentioned in the press. In *Making ADD Work*, Dr. Grossberg corrects this omission. It's a correction that those of us who have known the secret, positive side of ADD think is long overdue.

This book provides readers with a real look at adults with ADD and shows them how they can use their special talents to their advantage. It's a book I wish I'd had years ago when I was struggling through school. For people at any point of their professional career, the author offers advice and inspiration that will allow them to soar.

Foreword

When Dr. Grossberg invited me to write the foreword for this book, I was quite honored to help this project come to fruition. In my work as a psychotherapist specializing in adult ADD for nearly ten years and the director of www.addconsults.com, I am well aware of the struggles my clients face when making career decisions and the many challenges that workplace environments can present. Now, I have this wonderful resource that I can recommend to them.

Most adults with ADD have had a lifetime of difficulty dealing with self-defeating behaviors, less-than-stellar social skills, and low self-esteem. Career choices and work issues are no exception. The consequences of ADD symptoms such as distractibility, hyperactivity, and impulsivity cannot be ignored, but by the same token, these struggles are not always given proper attention because of the lack of concrete information available to both worker and employer.

ADD is most destructive when it remains undiagnosed, untreated, and misunderstood. Once I started seeing the transformations in my clients when they got a hold of clear, concise information on ADD, I was hooked. Armed with the insider's edge of *being* a professional with ADD, it soon became clear to me that learning all I could about ADD and teaching others was my calling. Knowing firsthand how this condition has impacted my own schooling, career choices, and work-place issues, I have wanted nothing more than to bring hope and re-lief to others. With that goal in mind, in addition to my private practice and online services, I've been on the ADDA (Attention Deficit Disorder Association) board of directors for seven years, serv-ing as its vice president for three of those years. I was coordinator for my local CHADD (Children and Adults with Attention-Deficit/ Hyperactivity Disorder) chapter for six years, during which I developed a support group for ADD adults.

All these venues have intimately contributed to my understand-ing of the common roadblocks that ADD adults encounter in mak-ing career choices and managing their condition at work, such as the following:

- Choosing careers that speak to their weaknesses rather than their strengths.

- Not knowing who or where to turn to for help.

- Chronic underachievement because of fears that advancement might be too overwhelming.

- Struggling with disorganization, procrastination, missed deadlines, and overcommitments.

- Not listening to their own inner rhythms and styles.

- Self-fulfilling prophecies of failure due to past experiences.

- Interpersonal relationship problems with co-workers and bosses.

The clinical golden rule when working with ADD adults is to suggest counseling, medication (when needed), support, and education, but in terms of support and education, there has been little written on the topic of ADD as related to career choices and work issues—until now. This book takes readers by the hand and leads them through the various mazes of how to find and utilize help to manage their ADD, whether it's working with an ADD coach or learning communication skills for the workplace.

Making ADD Work is written with such insight and warm understanding, it's as if the writer is standing behind your shoulder, gently pointing you in the right direction. Rather than spending a lot of time explaining and describing ADD, she shares stories of real people's struggles and successes, a refreshing change from the clichéd tips so often found in self-help books. Dr. Grossberg's gift is in helping readers find validation that they are not alone in facing these challenges while at the same time showing how possible it is to find the right career path and celebrate the journey to success. She intuitively understands the struggles while paving the way with no-nonsense, pragmatic, logically organized strategies. The inclusion of a summary of tips after each chapter is an added bonus and a wonderful way to review the chapters without having to reread them.

The book focuses on how to make ADD work to one's advantage, how to leverage it so that one can march forward, equipped with tools to make life easier. What I found particularly refreshing was the encouraging words from people who expressed how their ADD has actually helped them. Whether speaking of high energy levels, creativity, or being empathetic and compassionate, adults with ADD often overlook their many strengths. For example, many are entrepreneurs or at least entrepreneurial in spirit. The author expertly covers this fascinating topic in her chapter on successful adults who've found their career paths by stepping outside the box. She offers suggestions on how to find structure in what is typically an unstructured environment.

Success begins with self-knowledge, and this book grips the reader with illuminating moments of self-recognition right from the start: from the woman who needs to be physically active to increase her concentration at work to the business consultant who depends on daily meditation to clear his mind to become more productive. This is a book for the real world—for real people—not for academics who are looking for statistics on how many people with ADD succeed in blue collar vs. white collar jobs, but for those on the front lines who need pragmatic tools to help them solve real problems on a daily basis. Technological tools are also suggested to help with productivity, particularly for those who face difficulties with reading and writing.

As the book segues into seeking and finding outside support, the author describes how coaches and professional organizers can offer structure and guidance. She gives us an inside look at the detailed mechanisms of coaching and how it can help one stay on task and be more productive at work.

Thankfully, the book also covers specifics that are often overlooked in other books on ADD, for example, how to effectively work with a boss and co-workers. The author offers insights about whether or not to disclose one's ADD, a topic that comes up frequently in my own work with ADD adults, by carefully outlining the pluses and minuses of such a disclosure.

The last section covers a very important and often confusing topic: the legal rights of employees with ADD. Dr. Grossberg discusses what those rights are and how to make them work to one's advantage. I've found that many professionals in the field are often at a loss as to how to advise their clients when it comes to legal issues. In this case, the author does an excellent job of encouraging employees to make the workplace "work" for them before taking legal action.

I heartily endorse this wonderful book because it covers just about everything one needs to know about career and work issues when coupled with ADD challenges. The fact that the author has researched the topic extensively and has interviewed numerous ADD experts in the field adds a depth and solidity to this book that will ensure it a spot for years to come on the shelves of many physicians, therapists, coaches, educators, and others who routinely work with ADD adults. It will be at the top of my list of recommended reading for my clients, because I am confident that by the time readers turn the final page, they will be filled with hope and equipped with concrete solutions—an ideal combination.

Terry Matlen, M.S.W., A.C.S.W.
Birmingham, Michigan
Author of *Survival Tips for Women with AD/HD*
Psychotherapist, private practice
Director, ADD Consults
ADDA, board of directors

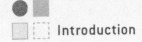

The Promise of Adult ADD

April earns more than $100,000 a year as a top-flight sales consultant and trainer in Texas. Fortune 500 clients consistently hire her because she is an unfailingly dynamic presenter. Her assistant has whipped April's office into meticulous shape: her filing system is color-coded, and she has a detailed daily to-do list. April jumps out of bed at 4 in the morning, and she can spend hours concentrating on tasks that interest her. But years after discovering that she has ADD, April still can't stop procrastinating if she finds a task dull. She's beat herself up about it and tried in vain to try to understand why she can't change her ways, but she remains a last-minute person too much of the time.

Rachel graduated from medical school to become an innovative psychiatrist and researcher. During her residency, however, her entire career was nearly derailed when she made a small mistake. She misread her schedule and erroneously left the hospital when she was on call—a definite taboo for medical residents. Fortunately, she had compassionate supervisors who encouraged her to get tested for ADD. They feared that she might have substance-abuse problems but wanted to be sure there wasn't another explanation for Rachel's seemingly inexplicable mistake. No one was more surprised than Rachel when the doctors who evaluated her told her she had the most clear-cut case of ADD they'd ever seen. Now, after learning how to work around her ADD, she asks her colleagues to read her schedules because she finds that she can't make sense of them, and she totes her laptop around the ward so she doesn't forget any of her tasks. She is a productive researcher and a compassionate clinician who understands that patients don't like to be seen only in light of their problems, but as well-rounded people.

Scott Eyre was pitching for the Toronto Blue Jays in a game against the Boston Red Sox when something indescribable overcame him. In less than two innings, he gave up nine runs and spaced out entirely on the mound. While Scott tried in vain to understand what had happened to him in the game, the team trainer urged him to get checked out for ADD. After receiving his diagnosis, Scott began taking medication to treat his ADD. His pitching has improved dramatically since then, and, now a relief pitcher for the San Francisco Giants, he is among the best pitchers in the Major League at stranding opposing runners on base.

April, Rachel, and Scott Eyre show the two-sided face of adult ADD. While incredibly gifted, they nonetheless experience problems with inattention, distractibility, and impulsiveness that have at times threatened to overwhelm their strengths. After they were diagnosed with ADD as adults, the long stream of apparently careless errors they'd been making their whole lives had a name. Even after they had an explanation for their behavior, they were still forced to come up with ways to prevent damaging mishaps and be productive.

This book is about the creative ways in which talented adults like April, Rachel, and Scott Eyre have found to conquer the obstacles that endangered their careers and to reach great professional success. Dozens of successful adults who are working effectively with ADD share their wisdom with you in these pages. They are CEOs, social workers, artists, professional athletes, writers, doctors, teachers, salespeople, lawyers, college professors, and entrepreneurs from all over the country. Through a process of trial and error that was often painful and sometimes fun, they spent years finding out how to leverage their strengths and overcome challenges. Their lives offer us food for thought and give us hope that adults with ADD can achieve success in their chosen fields.

Who Contributed to This Book

This book presents what successful ADD adults have learned through their own brave processes of seeking answers and organizes the information for you in manageable ways. You can turn to their hard-won insight over the course of your working life. You don't need to read everything at once; you can instead use this book as a trusty companion and consult the wisdom of these successful adults when an issue or problem arises in your work, or when you need the inspiration of people who have struggled with ADD and not just managed it but turned their ways of thinking and acting to work in their favor. Through the stories of ADD adults presented in this book, you can understand how to help yourself, your loved ones and colleagues, and the bright, creative people that make up about 5 percent of adults in this country.

Reading this book is like spending time at a support group with successful, helpful, adult "ADDers" who are willing to take the time to spell out exactly how they manage their daily lives. This is important because ADD is still very much a closet disorder, and adults with ADD are not always in close contact with people who can light their way toward more productive, happier lives. Many adults with ADD live in areas where there are no local support groups, and those who live in areas with support groups often do not have enough time in their busy lives to attend them.

The people featured in this book often did things instinctively for years—even before they knew they had ADD. For example, they color-coded their files, used alarms to remind them of meetings, and asked their bosses to give them clear project deadlines in writing. They followed these practices because they simply felt right—just like you may do—without really knowing why. After they were diagnosed with ADD, most of them as adults, they learned more about what helped them and grew to appreciate what made them different and even gave them advantages in certain arenas of the work world.

This book draws on their gifts, their courageous search for answers, and the knowledge of professionals who can help them. Their shared wisdom is intended to enable adults with ADD and those who love them to stop groping in the dark and learn the very real ways in which people have found success working with this condition, which is still unnecessarily called an all-around "disorder." Perhaps it's more fruitful and effective to think of ADD as a style of working and thinking that presents both negative attributes and positive qualities. The upsides of ADD don't exactly compensate for the negatives, but they do give ADD adults gifts that set them apart from the norm.

From the tips presented in this book, you can choose what makes sense and appeals to you, and, using your heightened sense of what's possible, you can also tweak the strategies offered here and make them your own. While reading this book, you may try a technique that works for you, mold a technique in a way that makes it better, or discover an entirely new technique.

For your information, this book uses the general term Attention

Deficit Disorder (ADD) to refer to both ADD and ADHD. There is no distinction made between adults who were diagnosed with ADD and those diagnosed with ADHD. The adults interviewed for this book ranged in age from thirty to sixty-four. They all received a diagnosis of ADD from a mental-health professional, which includes psychologists, psychiatrists, and other medical doctors.

How This Book Is Organized

This book breaks down the wealth of information from successful adults with ADD into three main areas:

- *Improving Your Work Skills:* How you can manage your life with ADD, get organized, stop procrastinating, boost your concentration, communicate effectively with co-workers and business contacts, and capitalize on your strengths.

- *Finding the Right Career Path:* How you can find a happy, healthy workplace where your talents can shine.

- *Getting Help:* How you can improve your work life with help from coaches, professional organizers, and career counselors and advocate for your rights and protections under the Americans with Disabilities Act (ADA).

About the Author

The ADD adults in this book told their stories to me, a career and educational consultant based in New York City. I've worked with adults and children with ADD and conducted original research into how to work effectively with this disorder. As a non-ADD adult, I appreciate the great balance that adults with ADD can bring to the workplace and to life. In a world where people tend to focus only on the possible, the insights of ADD individuals can help us see what at first seems impossible. If we think only in proscribed solution sets for any problem, we're not thinking smart. We can all learn from adults with ADD, and we need to help them manage their lives so that their special talents can be realized. As anyone who has spent time with an ADD child or adult knows, they tend to be insightful, creative, lively, and inspiring, and are without exception smarter than they know.

Read on to gather practical advice, inspiration, and hope for the estimated 8 million U.S. adults who have ADD and the countless others who suspect they do and may recognize themselves in these pages.

1

ADD at Work:
Opportunities and Challenges

*"I can multitask. I can get ready to face a hitter and make
conversation with a fan sitting right behind me."*
—SCOTT EYRE, SAN FRANCISCO GIANTS RELIEF PITCHER

■ Soaring with ADD

David Neeleman, the CEO of JetBlue Airways, and Scott Eyre,
relief pitcher for the San Francisco Giants, both have Attention
Deficit Disorder (ADD). David Neeleman brought his jets off the
ground and into the skies with a totally new model that no one
thought was possible—he made them comfortable, playful, and extremely profitable. While his airline has soared and has branched
into twenty-seven cities in recent years, the traditional carriers have
plunged into debt and are cutting flights. Pitcher Scott Eyre throws
jetlike fastballs at speeds that seem to approach the sound barrier.
Both of them are stars and are thriving with ADD—maybe even
partly because of it.

Their success goes against everything the wider world has been saying about ADD. Conventional wisdom says that this disorder, which
involves symptoms of inattention, hyperactivity, and impulsivity, is an

all-around disadvantage, and the efforts of the medical and mental-health community have been aimed at managing it, ironing it out, reducing its symptoms, and making adults with ADD look like everyone else.

But maybe there's another way to look at adult ADD.

Although ADD is generally a liability in the traditional school system, which tends to value attention, patience, and compliance, the work world rewards assets that school doesn't—including risk-taking and vision, energy, and creativity. The careers of successful ADD adults such as David Neeleman and Scott Eyre can help us re-examine this disorder. If we really want to come to a nuanced understanding of ADD, we have to ask how people like Neeleman and Eyre have managed their work lives to their advantage. Are they even causing us to question our basic assumptions about ADD? Is it time to stop thinking of ADD as simply a disorder? First, we'll talk about what ADD can look like at work and explore its two-sided nature that presents opportunities for enormous success while simultaneously presenting problems that can derail this success.

What Does ADD Look Like at Work?

There is no one "typical" case of ADD. Because it is a disorder of attention, it has the potential to affect you in many different ways over the course of the day and over your work life. It's the cause of phenomenal success and, simultaneously, of incomprehensible failure.

ADD at work can take many forms. It affects the entrepreneur who comes up with an incredibly innovative idea—one that has the potential to revolutionize an entire industry—but who can't implement the idea without a huge support staff to handle the details. It can affect the lawyer who can't file papers but who devises a brilliant courtroom strategy at 3 A.M. on the night before the case goes before the judge. ADD can also explain the behavior of the corporate trainer who can't possibly fathom what she's going to say until she's before an audience of 100 people and suddenly comes alive with a speech that's by turns brilliant, funny, and right on target. ADD is then a kind of "Swiss cheese" disorder in which great strengths co-exist with persistent problems. It's not an all-around disorder but causes large gaps or problems in the midst of remarkable talents.

Here are some ways in which ADD can manifest itself in your daily work life:

- You have a schedule filled with unfinished to-dos and endless procrastination. You just can't work until the heat is on.

- You have a cluttered desk and workspace whose organization has no rhyme or reason. Things that are out of sight are truly out of mind.

- You juggle a constant stream of projects that lose their appeal after the eureka moment during which you created them has passed.

- You keep working on projects until they're perfect, which means they never end.

- You are bothered by the constant, nagging feeling that you're about to get fired or that you never measure up to your boss's—or your own—expectations.

- Sometimes, you can't start projects at work even though you really want to.

- You have a troubled history of saying the wrong thing to the wrong person—even though it seemed right at the time.

- Unfinished sentences, books, and e-mails follow you everywhere. Your attention turns off mid-stream, and you can't push yourself to finish things.

- You are besieged daily with ideas about what you'd rather be doing and where you'd rather be; as a result, you always feel on edge or restless.

- You don't know how you get from A to Z, and you can't explain it to anyone else.

- You know deep down that you're smarter and better than what your work reflects.

At the same time that you may suffer from some of the problems mentioned above, you may also find that you have the following areas of strength:

- You come up with ideas that no one else seems to think of, and you may also have too many talents and bright ideas to engage all of them.

- You have the ability to focus on things that interest you for many hours without heeding your hunger or the clock.

- You are the life of the party and never seem to have a dull thought or moment.

- You can marshal unbounded energy for projects that interest you. After your co-workers are flagging, you are still going strong.

- You can jump right into something without planning—and function very well.

• Change doesn't scare you, and, in fact, you embrace it whole-heartedly.

• You may be open to working with others because they can balance what you have to offer and can help you see your great ideas through to fruition.

• You are compassionate and empathic; people in pain don't scare you because you understand how they feel.

■ What Adult ADD Is Not

• *Adult ADD doesn't create fidget monsters.* ADD in adults does not usually resemble the prototypical symptom of the childhood form of the disorder—constant restlessness. The common misperception about children with ADD is that they are constantly squirming, and this also characterizes many people's ideas about adults with the disorder. However, as adults age, their restless symptoms tend to wane, while their problems with inattention continue to complicate their lives. Add the increased responsibilities of adult life, including a job, a family, and finances, and you can create a recipe for persistent problems. Adult ADD is not a disorder that reveals itself to the world directly through squirming and fidgeting, but, for those who deal with it daily, it can be an insidious foe, threatening to unravel their careers and throw their work life off track.

• *ADD does not mean definite failure.* Although ADD undoubtedly complicates people's work lives, it need not be a death sentence or a reason to predict certain failure. With smart work skills, the selection of a suitable workplace, and help from others who know about this disorder, adults with ADD can be incredibly successful. ADD in adulthood is as much a promise as it is a challenge—it means using your strengths to overcome your problems and claim the success that can be yours.

- *ADD is not cured by popping a pill.* Although there are pharmacological treatments for ADD (see Chapter 3 for more information), most adults with this disorder find that taking medicine doesn't immediately clear up all their work problems. They still need to learn how to organize their tasks and time and how to find a workplace that calls on their talents and skills. That's where this book can help.

Taking Real Steps

Although researchers know a lot more about ADD in adults than they did only a decade ago, we're still struggling to understand this disorder and how it plays out over the life span. This book doesn't claim to be the ultimate authority on these lingering questions. What it does instead is look at how adults are working productively with ADD in the midst of their continuing quest to find answers and to understand fully the way in which the ADD brain looks and works. This book is written for people who've already received a professional diagnosis of ADD, and it doesn't cover how to diagnose or to pharmacologically treat the condition. Many adults with ADD also have co-existing emotional and learning issues that need the treatment of professionals. Consult the Helpful Resources section at the end of the book to find professionals in your area if you feel you need this type of assistance.

While we can't today claim to understand ADD entirely, we can understand the steps people have taken to deal with it in the workplace. These steps are incredibly valuable and real—as are the successes and special contributions of ADD adults.

• ● • CHAPTER HIGHLIGHTS • ● •

▪ This book offers a menu of options that have worked well for adults with ADD. Use your heightened sense of what's possible to choose what's right for you. You can also experiment and develop an entirely new technique or path.

▪ The first section of this book will help you satisfy your curiosity about what has helped other people improve their work skills, and it may also help you put together into a neater package the things you've already been doing to manage your career and to evaluate whether your strategies are working for you.

▪ Real stories of ADD adults challenge conventional wisdom about this condition. ADD adults can be remarkably successful if they find a career that calls on their very real strengths in a workplace that's right for them.

▪ While researchers are still trying to understand ADD in adults and we don't know everything we could about how ADD plays itself out over the adult life span, we do know about real steps others have taken to improve their work life, and you can, too.

●●● **PART 1**

Improving Your Work Skills

2

Getting Organized and Managing Your Time

> *"Managing ADD is a lot like trying to be physically fit by working out and watching what you eat every day. ADD isn't like pneumonia, where you take a pill and it goes away. You've really got to try to manage it and structure your life around it."*
>
> —JEFF, COMPUTER SALESPERSON

Recognizing What Works For You

You've managed your symptoms and discovered ways to get your work done since childhood. You may have found that you were more productive when you did your homework at the kitchen table instead of working alone in your room, and you also knew that you needed to take frequent breaks while writing a long paper. You may have found that you could pay more attention in the classes you had after recess, while you couldn't focus during the first class in the morning.

You knew these things inside perhaps without putting them together into a coherent set of guidelines, but you may not have told anyone about them because your insights sounded strange. If everyone else could get through algebra class at 9 in the morning, why couldn't you? Why did you get lost in your own thoughts when everyone else seemed to be paying attention? Your fear of rejection and shame may have prevented you from having an open dialogue about how you worked best, and you may have kept others and even yourself from putting all these life and work strategies together. You may also not have found receptive teachers or colleagues who accepted the ways you worked best.

If you think about it, there are most likely things you've done that have worked well for you in the past. Figuring out how and when you work best is even more important in adulthood, when you are faced with the competing demands of family and work life without a lot of the structure that accompanies childhood. As an adult, there are many warring claims on your time and energy, and you have to know how to handle all your responsibilities and get your work done.

Adults with ADD discover strategies as they go along in life while battling the obstacles in their path. They can overcome amazingly daunting challenges by using techniques that they improvise on the spot using their great powers of innovation and creativity. Let's look at the story of one brave woman who went from high-school dropout to disabilities lawyer and see how she handled the seemingly overwhelming challenges that nearly prevented her from living out her dream.

■ Katherine's Story: From High-School Dropout to Lawyer

Anyone looking at her today would never guess that Katherine was a high-school dropout. She hasn't followed the traditional career trajectory. While the other students at her prestigious law school had attended Ivy League colleges, Katherine overcame a dismal high-school career in a low-income area of Hollywood, California, during which she failed out of school and had to go on to complete her degree later.

She sailed through grammar school, but in the seventh grade, her grades took a nose-dive. She started to get into trouble, and school began to turn her off entirely. Her grammar and spelling were horrible, and she became a C and D student. No one could figure her out. She couldn't read or memorize, and she didn't have study skills; instead, she would just look at end-of-chapter summaries and try to get by on exams. She never read children's books and only got as far as Algebra I in math. In high school, she missed most of the education, but no one thought of doing an assessment to figure out if Katherine had a learning disability that was preventing her from reaching her true potential.

After getting her high school diploma through a G.E.D. course, Katherine became a hairdresser. She was so restless at that time that she couldn't sit still for more than half an hour. Boredom would overtake her, and she'd have to start moving. She couldn't stay in a job for longer than a year, and her mind was continuously spinning. No one thought she could do much of anything. Completely demoralized, she took several years to get to college. She found her way to a community college and was then diagnosed with dyslexia. She wound up graduating from a four-year college as a creative writing major with great grades. She applied and was accepted to a prestigious law school. Although she had high LSAT scores, she believes that she only got into school because she applied through the disabilities office and the school wanted her for reasons of diversity.

Right before her first year of law school, she was finally diagnosed with ADD and began taking Ritalin. Twenty minutes after taking her first dose, she had the surreal experience of being able to concentrate for the first time in her life. Although her medication helped her focus, her first semester of law school was still a struggle.

Faced with a vast amount of reading and writing, Katherine was sure she'd flunk out of school. Doubts about her competence continued to dog her, and she felt isolated from the other students because she had to leave the campus right after class and study at home so she could concentrate.

The first year of law school is difficult enough for the average student, but Katherine faced the academic equivalent of climbing Mount Everest. Using her preternatural powers of innovation, she scrambled to develop techniques that would get her through her coursework. She was not only diligent but creative in solving any problem that came her way. In addition to studying nearly twenty-four hours a day, she bought all her books on tape because she couldn't get through the reading. To make the material comprehensible, she graphed everything in PowerPoint because she couldn't produce a traditional outline. After she passed her first semester, she knew she would graduate.

Right after law school, she devised a program to offer legal services for children with learning disabilities, and her novel ideas resulted in a grant and later a fellowship. Today, she represents low-income families whose children have ADD and other learning disabilities to help them get assessments and services from their school districts.

Katherine's struggle to manage her ADD symptoms continues today; for example, she knows she doesn't have the luxury to delay working on her cases until the last minute. She starts organizing her work and breaking it down into discrete smaller steps as soon as it's been assigned to her. If she has a lot to do, her mind starts spinning, and her solution is to make herself extremely organized. If you visited her at her West Coast office, you'd find her there late at night when it's quiet and less distracting.

Katherine's work environment is very supportive of her. Her boss knows about Katherine's ADD and has provided her with technological aids such as computer programs that read back to her, and her colleagues proofread her written work.

Katherine's story shows that sometimes ADD adults actually work better at more rather than less complex jobs. For example, Katherine says she could never handle the details of being a paralegal but that being a lawyer is perfect for her because she is "more big picture than details—law fits into the way I think on five levels at the same time." This position is the first she's held for more than a year because she's designed it to be fun, and she does several things at once, including teaching and bringing outreach programs to the community.

It's clear that Katherine has changed her life trajectory through smart work skills. After many years of struggling to access her true skills, she was finally able to find a way to overcome the dyslexia and ADD that made it difficult for her to see and use her strengths. Her life is a testament to her courage and her willingness to keep fighting to find the path that was right for her, even after years of false starts and wrong turns.

Katherine's story is one among many that challenge the wisdom about working with ADD. Until recently, experts in the field believed that children grew out of their ADD symptoms when they turned eighteen, but now we know that these symptoms don't disappear when people get their driver's licenses—they only change into more subtle, less noticeable forms that may escape the notice of mental-health professionals. The current-day conventional wisdom is that ADD is a handicap in adults, and that adults with this condition aren't likely to succeed at complex jobs like Katherine's. She and many others are proving conventional wisdom wrong every day.

■ Adding Skills to Your Personal Repertoire

Adults with ADD are a lot like chefs who are very comfortable in the kitchen. They don't follow recipes because they've made the dishes so many times before. Through experimentation, they determined the optimum amount of salt to make their pasta boil and the right amount of sugar to add to the tomato sauce. An observer watching them cook might regard the process as haphazard, but it's actually been fine-tuned by long years of experience and a number of ruined dinners that had to be tossed away and started anew.

If the observer were to ask the chef how he or she gets the pasta sauce to taste so succulent, the ADD chef might be at a loss for words. "I don't know," he or she would say. I just add salt and—"

"But how much salt?" the curious observer might want to know.

"I don't know exactly—just the amount of salt to make things turn out right."

Like seasoned chefs, adults with ADD may not be able to step back and analyze everything they do that makes their days run smoothly and that works around their deficits. They've been doing these things for a long time, and they may do them without even realizing it.

The first step to modifying your existing repertoire is to examine fully what it is you do well and what is working for you or has worked in the past. In this process, it helps to take into account what sets you apart from the pack. Rather than getting down on yourself for your differences, it may be more fruitful to look at your differences and see how they can be strengths. Pick and choose from the strategies used by other adults with an eye toward what makes sense for you and what builds on your already established productive ways of working.

■ Remember That You Do Things Well— and Differently

Tom's story may help remind you of how to appreciate your particular ways of working, even if they don't seem "normal" by others' standards. Now the director of development at a prominent graduate school, Tom remembers that as a kid, he couldn't read well and was sent to a learning specialist. Instead of making him feel self-conscious or stupid for his tendency to read down instead of across columns of text, this woman told Tom that in China, he would be able to read very well indeed! Tom took this lesson to heart, and he offers it as advice to other adults with ADD. "I realized at that moment that although I'm different, there's no badness in the way my brain is wired," he says.

Since childhood, Tom has chosen to do things his own way, and the method by which he raises money from donors in his director of development position isn't orthodox. Instead of asking for gifts outright, he waits for people to tell him their dreams and wishes, and he helps facilitate them. Using his creative, unique method, he has closed multimillion-dollar gifts for his school.

As you look at the way you do things, remember that no one can do everything well. You may want to work with a manager, friend, coach, or therapist to prioritize the areas you want to work on first. Many adults with ADD have a personal history of feeling down about themselves and beating themselves up internally for what they feel they don't do well, so it helps to realize that you have areas of strength and don't need to make wholesale changes in your personality or work style.

April, a sales consultant in Texas who works with Fortune 500 companies and makes more than $100,000 per year, has for years tried to avoid procrastinating. Although she has instituted a sophisticated tickler file, and her extremely organized assistant (who also has ADD) produces a daily list of her boss's every task, April still can't avoid saving things for the last minute. She finds herself at a loss to explain why she can't make her brain work differently, but over the years, she has decided that it's okay to have a few sticking points, as long as she's accomplishing what she wants to in the end.

Tom, the director of development at a graduate school, still misses some donor meetings due to his less-than-ideal time-management skills, but he's learned to forgive himself for this, and rather than getting into a blaming game with others or himself, he has just accepted that occasional misses are part of his work game plan. Although he can be a bit disorganized, he is nonetheless very productive and has delivered a number of large gifts to his university.

▓ Establishing Priorities About What You Want to Change

When you look over this chapter and read about the kinds of self-management strategies that have helped other adults with ADD, keep in mind the things you want to fix now. Changing the way you work is an evolving process, and if you can make it as natural to you as possible, there's a better chance it will actually stick. Choosing strategies that fit in with the way you currently work will be easier because they will involve a lesser amount of change.

When clients start working with Becca Gross, an ADD coach based in Massachusetts, she asks them about strategies that have worked well for them in the past—even briefly—and she digs for information that they already have about themselves. "After they're diagnosed with ADD, many people want to organize away and plan major strategies," she says. "It's more useful to look for what's working now and build on it and change as little as possible."

Organizational and Time-Management Tools

A Note on Planning

Having a calendar is one thing—using it is entirely another. Many ADD adults report having set up a perfectly tenable day timer or calendar but not using it. Therefore, it may be useful to contract with a friend, co-worker, or coach to remind you to check in with your calendar on a regular basis, at least until doing so becomes second nature to you.

According to New York City professional organizer Sondra Schiff, who has worked extensively with ADD adults, "It's hard for 'ADDers' to acquire a concrete sense of time—that there's a beginning, middle, and end. They often use their calendar as a pad and don't register days and hours." She works with her clients to look at specific days with a heightened awareness that the day only has fixed amount of time.

Many ADD adults are so energetic and inventive that they plan too ambitiously. Sara, an artist and singer/songwriter in Dallas, describes herself "as an A-plus. I always want things I do to be soaring through the roof. What I write down to do in half a day, others write down for a week," she says. "I've learned to say, 'in this amount of time, I can do fabulous but not superfabulous.'" She now feels a greater sense of accomplishment because she realizes that she's completed a lot, even if she hasn't attacked everything on her lengthy to-do list.

Many adults who've tried a variety of planning devices also find that it helps to simplify and streamline their systems. Brian, an independent IT consultant, admits he's "a gadget freak. I'm on my fourth Palm Pilot," he says. But he claims that it's best to "pick one method of planning. If you're not organized and consistent, it won't help you to have four different types. If you're all over the place, it doesn't help."

Veterans of the planning process have found that the best planning systems are a bit fluid. Jeff, the computer salesman, knows that creating a calendar does not in itself mean that he is going to accomplish everything he writes down and that he should realize that unforeseen events will often get in the way. Therefore, you should forgive yourself if you don't accomplish everything you set out to do. Jeff makes daily lists with about twelve tasks, but he doesn't get ruffled if he only does three due to the intervention of unpredicted, more important events such as new client opportunities that disrupt his planned schedule.

Rachel, the psychiatrist, makes her daily schedule flexible. "I have to be available and can't tell people to go away and come back tomorrow," she says. "So I build flexibility into my schedule. I will put 'writing' in for five days. If it doesn't happen one day, it's not a big deal."

Good planning and an improved sense of how long projects actually take are the grease that makes your daily schedule run smoothly. Katherine, the one-time high-school dropout who became a lawyer practicing in the area of disabilities, knows that, unlike some of her colleagues, she "can't have the luxury of waiting to do something." She stops the "spinning in my head" by tackling things right away if she begins to feel overwhelmed. She uses her calendar to break every large task into smaller steps and then to sort out when she's going to accomplish these bite-size chunks of work. "I can't take a short-cut," she admits.

Taming the Paper Tiger

Caitlin, a Philadelphia lawyer with ADD who has practiced in the paper-intensive area of litigation for more than twenty years, claims that she "still hasn't tamed the paper tiger." Many of the ADD adults I interviewed for this book found dealing with paper problematic and had dedicated a lot of their strong creative energies to figuring out how to deal with it.

Color-coded systems are a common tool that slays the tiger. April, the Texas sales consultant, works with an assistant who also has ADD. They have instituted a color-coded filing system that uses glaring red files for special projects and more muted green files for regular business matters. This intuitive color system helps April immediately visually key in to what the paper in each folder represents. April also has set up a large wall calendar, and seeing the dates when her work is due helps her absorb this information.

ADD adults sometimes have trouble remembering where they have filed certain papers and which category they've put a receipt in. For example, they may not remember if they filed the receipt from the business lunch they had with their lawyer under "lawyer" or "restaurant." Coaches suggest that you cue your files so that if you look for the receipt under "restaurant," a note in the file will direct you to your "lawyer" file.

Vanessa, a New York City public school teacher, uses a color highlighter to read and write in her books. While this tactic is generally a no-no in school, it helps her keep track of her ideas and her progress through the book.

Professional organizer Laura Lakin of New York City says that some people like to put papers away in closed filing cabinets, while "a whole other kind of person will panic if he or she cannot see paper. It's okay to be like that." She suggests to such clients that they purchase rolling carts at office-supplies stores. Letter- or legal-size files fit right into the cart, and you can label the files with large tags that make them immediately recognizable. Lakin says this kind of filing system works particularly well for people who are visually oriented.

Many ADD adults generate so many great ideas on a daily level that their brains feel besieged. ADD coach Jennifer Koretsky, who's based in New York City, suggests that people with an infusion of good ideas write them down and store them away so they don't look at them everyday. She suggests coming back to them over time. To capture your good ideas, you may want to supplement your day timer with a notebook of any variety that makes sense to you.

Other ADD adults have devised paper systems that channel their thoughts by engaging and capturing all their streams of thought at one time. Katherine, the lawyer who advocates for children with learning disabilities, divides her legal pad into three columns. While she's in a meeting, she takes notes on what's going on and also leaves room on the page to take notes about whatever pops into her head unbidden. Writing down the irrelevant things that leap into her head helps her focus and preserve her important thoughts on unrelated topics for a later time when she's ready to look at them. See Chapter 10 to find out more about the services of professional organizers who can help you get your physical space in order.

Outside Accountability

The third part of this book deals with how you can enlist the help of others to achieve success in your work. Many adults with ADD involve others in the management of their work to keep themselves accountable and on track. Aaron, a New York–based lighting designer, for example, found that he works best when he can get clarity from his boss about what he needs to do. On jobs where his supervisor's directions were diffuse or vague, he felt confused about how to prioritize his work.

Vanessa, the public school teacher, sends out newsletters to her students' parents, telling them when they can expect to have their children's grades sent home. This helps her produce the report cards on time—something she's struggled with in the past—because she has set a deadline with the outside world. ADD coaches can also help you remain accountable; for more information on coaches, see Chapter 10.

Entrepreneurs often find it useful to hire others to keep them on track. Many hire assistants or professionals such as accountants to handle the paperwork they don't like or have time for. For example, April, the sales consultant, has hired an assistant, lawyer, and accountant to help her manage her business, and she has found their assistance invaluable. For more information on entrepreneurs, see Chapter 8.

Calendars, Timers, and Reminders

Many adults with ADD impose structure on their work lives through the use of reminder systems. There is a whole world of reminders, and the one you choose has to fit your needs and your desired level of discretion. You may work in the kind of environment in which a buzzer or beeper won't be disruptive or embarrassing, but if this isn't the case, you may opt for a visual reminder system.

If you enter a stationery store, you will find endless calendars and day timers that measure off every second of your existence. The important thing, many successful adults with ADD suggest, is to make whatever system you choose your own. For your purposes, a $5 daily journal may work as well as a $150 leather-bound multi-section book.

Vanessa, now a New York City public school teacher with ADD, started using day timers in college because she felt as though she was floating through life and never knew what was going to come next. Day timers helped her sort out her work and feel more on track, and they helped her salvage her at-first shaky college career and graduate from her competitive college with decent grades.

When she first started using a day timer and reminder lists, however, Vanessa often put too much on her to-do list. She came up with two-page typed lists that made her feel overwhelmed. Now, she limits her list to a few critical things so she doesn't feel so burdened. She also uses other people to keep her schedule on track. While giving classroom lessons, Vanessa finds that she often speaks for too long and runs into the time that she has allotted for the children's independent work, so she appoints a student in her class as the time-keeper. She also uses a ten-minute timer to keep her lessons on schedule and sets an alarm on her PDA, or personal digital assistant, to remind her to take her medication or to attend irregular events such as meetings at work.

Scott Eyre, a left-handed relief pitcher for the San Francisco Giants, uses a Palm Pilot to remind him of his appointments. "I bring it everywhere, even to the field," he says. He also constantly writes himself little notes. "I used to forget to leave my brother tickets in the box office, but now I make a note and go right to the ticket counter when I arrive at the stadium."

Rachel, a psychiatrist with ADD, uses the calendar on her computer's Outlook system to plan in advance for due dates. She enters the start date when she should begin working on every project and then enters a due date that is several days before the actual due date. She keeps the actual due date stored elsewhere so she doesn't panic if she misses a self-created due date.

A simple digital watch with an alarm can remind you of appointments and responsibilities during the day. There are also watches with lots of bells and whistles—should you want them. One such device, the WatchMinder, was invented by a child psychologist named Laurence D. Becker, Ph.D., to facilitate time-management, training, and behavior change. This digital watch uses a vibration system (you feel it but don't hear it, so it's private) and visual prompts to remind you to take your medication, check e-mail, go to work, go to your coach, pay bills, and about seventy other customizable commands. You can preprogram up to sixteen reminder alarms per day into the watch to keep your day on track. You can even use it to remind you to be positive and relax at certain intervals during the day—even every five minutes. Its face is broad and the screen easy to read. Call 1-800-961-0023 or visit www. watchminder.com for more information.

Technological Tools

Many successful adults with ADD have used technological tools to reduce distractions and to more effectively manage their time. The tools included here were tried by ADD adults, who found them useful and worth the price.

Driving software. When faced with a road trip—whether a family vacation or a business meeting that requires driving—many adults with ADD have difficulty getting directions in advance and accurately anticipating the time it will take to arrive at their destinations. Devices called Magellan GPS feature mapping software and portable global positioning systems that facilitate driving. Rather than printing out a series of written directions or carrying a glove compartment full of unwieldy fold-up maps, you can position a Magellan GPS in your car that tells you exactly how to arrive at your destination *as you drive.* Far superior to the backseat driver who doesn't know where he's going, the Magellan system navigates your route and gives you voice and visual prompts at every turn. It also features a full-color display so you can see your route. This type of software has been a lifesaver for traveling salespeople and others who have to drive to see their clients.

The Magellan GPS lets you know where you are at any given moment, your speed, and the distance and time until you reach your destination. This will help you avoid speeding tickets and give you ample time to call ahead if you think you may arrive late for your meeting. If you encounter traffic or a road block en route to your destination, the system will plan out an alternate route for you. It will guide you to restaurants, hotels, gas stations, and points of interest along the way. The company also makes lightweight handheld devices equipped with mapping systems. Call 1-800-707-9971 or visit www.magellangps.com for information and prices.

Noise-canceling headphones. The Bose Quiet Comfort® acoustic noise-canceling headphones identify and reduce undesirable noise before it enters your ears, allowing more of the music, words, or silence you desire to reach you. The headphones have an ergonomic, lightweight design. You can wear them for writing, reading, and concentrating in loud places, accompanied by music of your choice or by the sounds of silence. The earphones cost about $199; visit www.bose.com for more information.

• ● • CHAPTER HIGHLIGHTS • ● •

▪ Examine your existing strategies and skills or things that have worked well for you in the past. Make additions and subtractions where you think they're necessary, remembering that you do things differently and keeping in mind what you do well.

▪ Changing the way you work is a gradual process, and adults with ADD have found it useful to figure out what has worked for them in the past and build on those strategies rather than changing everything at once. Remember, sometimes the best piece of advice is that "if it ain't broke, don't fix it."

▪ Just because you have a calendar, that doesn't mean you'll use it consistently. At least initially, you may need to rely on friends or

Software for Writing and Reading

If you don't like to type or write, Dragon Naturally Speaking software programs can help. You can work with your Windows program by only using your voice and without touching the keyboard, or by using a combination of voice, keyboard, and mouse. The program allows you to dictate an e-mail message to send out over the Internet and to read aloud numbers from a spreadsheet and enter them by voice into a database. After entering the data, you can format it and activate pull-down menus and initiate other commands by voice. The program also enables you to dictate at speeds up to 160 words per minute and saves transcription costs.

Another software program that reads for you is called Kurzweil 3000, which works with both Macintosh and PC platforms. This type of program can be particularly helpful for ADD adults who are also dyslexic or who have problems reading and seeing text. The software speaks letters and words as you type and identifies spelling mistakes and incorrect words. The program enables you to see, hear, and highlight sections of the text, thereby increasing your comprehension. You can have the program read back your writing to be sure it makes sense and to facilitate proofreading. You can also create audio files to listen to on portable players. The software, which has color and black-and-white versions, is available in various packages at different prices; the black-and-white software for individual use was around $1,000 at the time of publication, while the color software cost about $1,500. You also need to purchase an Epson scanner so you can scan your reading materials. For more information, call 1-800-894-5374 or visit www.kurzweiledu.com.

Adults with ADD have found that the assistive devices in this chapter have facilitated their work and allowed them to maneuver around their obstacles to be able to leverage their strengths. Chapter 5 discusses ADD strengths and how to use them to your advantage in the work world.

colleagues to remind you to check your calendar or planning system on a regular basis.

■ "Taming the paper tiger" can be difficult for ADD adults. It may help to color-code files, create rolling carts with papers out in the open, or devise special note-taking systems that allow you to engage many streams of thought at once. Your personal choice of filing system can and should reflect your idiosyncrasies and accommodate your particular brand of genius.

■ Making yourself accountable to other people may help you keep your work on track; therefore, whenever possible, you should set realistic deadlines and announce them in advance to co-workers or clients.

■ Many adults with ADD find it very helpful to rely on calendars or other reminder systems. Whether you're using a day planner, a personal digital assistant, or a watch with an alarm, make your chosen system your own and avoid overly ambitious planning. Good planning and an improved sense of how long projects actually take are the grease that makes your daily schedule work. Fancy bells and whistles cannot take the place of wise and realistic time management.

■ Technological tools such as noise-canceling headsets, satellite-based driving systems, and dictation and writing software have helped ADD adults. These are particularly helpful for adults who may also have reading or writing problems.

3

Maintaining Your Concentration

"I can get into an anxious spiral and can't concentrate. Trying to work when I can't can damage my confidence."
—PHIL, SCREENWRITER

Focusing Your Mind

Adults with ADD often find that their levels of concentration are affected by their physical states. Many describe the close relationship between their minds and bodies. If they don't sleep enough or don't consistently take their medication, they discover that their work suffers as a result.

For example, when Sara, the singer/songwriter and artist in Texas, has racing thoughts at night, she doesn't enjoy a deep, restful sleep. On these fitful nights, she says, "My brain is buzzing away with a million ideas—I'm building cities in my mind." If her restless sleep continues for several nights, she experiences a weakened ability to filter distractions during the day, and she has to modify her surroundings to diminish the interruptions and be able to concentrate.

The regular scheduling of meals also boosts long-term concentration. Aaron, a lighting designer who used to work on-site at building projects, found that he would begin to "hyperfocus," or enter a narrowed channel of concentration in which his attention was only focused on the task at hand. In this state, he would forget to eat lunch, and his hunger actually worsened his ability to focus as the day wore on. He found that his concentration improved when he built lunchtime into his daily schedule, even if it meant disrupting his work. This chapter presents strategies that adults with ADD have used to boost their concentration, reduce their restlessness, and focus on their work.

■ Physical Movement

Physical movement can be a great boon to concentration. Caitlin, the lawyer, whips around the half-mile circuit surrounding her office in Philadelphia when she can't concentrate or when she feels stressed to the point of overload. Many successful adults with ADD have built regular exercise into their schedules, which they find is advantageous in helping them focus.

Once they're on the job, however, many adults with ADD find that it helps them concentrate if they restrict excessive movements. Sean, an international business consultant in the Boston area, tries to keep himself chained to his desk because his first inclination is to jump around and even feel tempted to hop on a plane to another country. He tells the oft-repeated urban legend about an ADD man who got himself to finish his work by closing his office door and stripping down to his underwear. This man knew he wouldn't leave his office and would get his work done if he had to appear in the hallway in his boxers.

Phil, a screenwriter, finds it useful to take a break while working. "I can get into an anxious spiral and can't concentrate," he says. "Trying to work when I can't can damage my confidence." Although stepping back from his work allows Phil to break this pernicious cy-cle, he can get so involved in other activities that he doesn't return to his work. "When I'm working on something I don't want to work on, other things that might not be as attention-grabbing be-come more enticing," he says, "so you have to be aware of the dan-ger of getting pulled in and getting 'hyperfocused.' I've taken a break and started to watch a movie and gotten sucked into it. I can go to another room as long as I can get myself back because transi-tions are hard."

Phil suggests working for a few minutes and then "giving your-self a recreational activity that your attention is naturally drawn to." While working on his screenplays, he goes to the Web to read news articles for a short time. "You're leavening the work experience by building in shorter-term rewards." But he warns against "giving yourself a pass on wasting a huge amount of time."

■ Finding a Quiet Space

Many successful ADD adults also get up with the roosters or, alter-natively, burn the midnight oil to find peaceful, quiet times to carry out their tasks that require intense concentration, especially writing. For example, Rosa, a screenwriter in Los Angeles, gets up early in the morning to do her writing. Usually up at 6 in the morning, she's already written for three hours by the time the rest of the world is up and starts disturbing her with phone calls. April, the wildly suc-cessful Texas sales consultant, gets out of bed at 4 A.M. to work in her home office and to complete work without being interrupted by her family or the phone. Jeff, the computer salesman, works at home several days a week, where his only interruption is his dog begging to go out.

ADD adults work best when they control interruptions to their concentration. Caitlin, a lawyer, has worked out a system where she closes her door as a barrier against the interruptions of her office, and she lets her calls go directly to voicemail if she's in the middle of working on a brief. "My clients get frustrated with getting voice mail," she says, "but I can't have the phone ringing, or I'd never get any work done." She returns calls at certain points during the day when she's taken a natural break from her work. Katherine, a disabilities lawyer, goes to a conference room in her office to avoid distractions and to work where it's quieter.

■ Medication

Although some ADD adults have found medication for their condition useful, many find that it only works for a limited time and then peters out or that it causes significant side effects, such as anxiety or insomnia, that outweigh its benefits. Some adults aren't helped by medication at all.

This book does not cover all the possible medications that treat some of the symptoms of adult ADD; for complete information, you should consult your doctor. However, medication can be an integral part of the approach many successful adults with ADD have taken to their work and personal lives.

Finding the right medication is an individualized process that presents difficulties for many ADD adults. Says Howard, a lawyer with ADD, "The problem with all stimulants is that they make my mind race in a way that impairs my quality of thinking. You can concentrate better, but you don't think as well. Also, even at smallest doses, they interfere with my sleep—even if I take them in the morning. If I'm not sleeping well, the adverse effect of sleep deprivation more than counterbalances the effect of the medication."

Howard is one of countless ADD adults who find that medication isn't a cure-all and whose struggle to treat this condition continues.

Others have found that medication is a great help to their ability to concentrate. When Vanessa, a New York City public school teacher, started taking stimulant medication, the effect was striking to her. "I make an analogy with asthma," she says. "When I was treated for asthma as an undergraduate, I knew what it was to breathe for the first time. Before taking ADD medication, I didn't know what life could be like." Prior to taking medication, she had felt anxious, overwhelmed, and out of control in a classroom with twenty students. Immediately after taking her medication, she noticed that she was more relaxed with the children in her class and didn't feel overstimulated. She says her medication has helped her be more patient with her students and better able to put on mental "blinders" that allow her to work with one child without being distracted by what else is going on in her classroom.

Even for those adults who've been greatly helped by medication, taking their drugs didn't entirely mitigate their problems. "ADD isn't like pneumonia," says Jeff, a computer salesman. "Medication helps, but you've also got to structure your life around having ADD."

Caitlin, the lawyer, says that "it's not like you can take a pill every day to cure ADD. It's a daily challenge to figure out what works best." Caitlin, who's in her late forties, believes that her life would have been easier if she'd been diagnosed earlier. But because she was diagnosed in her forties, her work patterns have already been established. She believes that her medication doesn't entirely overcome her long-established work patterns.

• ⦿ • CHAPTER HIGHLIGHTS • ⦿ •

■ ADD adults report that there is a close connection between being able to focus and their physical state. For example, lack of sleep lessens their ability to concentrate. They are also helped to concentrate by making time for meals in the midst of work.

Meditation

Meditation has helped some ADD adults slow down their minds and concentrate better. Sean, an international business consultant, lives life on the go; he is bubbling over with energy, and he's always ready with a witty story—a talent he ascribes to his Irish-Catholic upbringing and the tradition of the great bar tale. His career has involved jumping on planes at the spur of the moment to travel to far-flung countries. His life has included a number of travel adventures, including being stuck in Latin America during a coup, and he has used his dynamic personality to build his company into a $150,000-per-year business. However, he says one of the greatest vacations he took was his trip several years ago to a meditation retreat. He still practices meditation today, and he credits it with slowing down his mind and allowing him to concentrate more on spiritual rather than material things.

Jennifer Koretsky, an ADD coach based in New York City, suggests to her clients, especially those who are brimming over with ideas, that they take time to recharge every day, which could mean meditating, taking a long walk, or taking a bath. "It has a ripple effect," she says, "and allows you to spend time in the present. It allows you to control your mind and the bombardment of thoughts."

- Although physical activity can actually calm the brain and improve concentration, some adults with ADD have found that they have to restrict their movements to get work done. A possibly apocryphal tale tells of a man who stripped down to his underwear to be sure he stayed in his office and completed his work.

- Build in carefully planned breaks that give your mind the chance to wander for a few minutes without going so long that you won't be able to return to the task at end.

- Finding a quiet time before the rest of the world is awake or after everyone has gone to bed and a quiet place can greatly help you concentrate.

- Medication is not a cure-all; it works differently for each ADD adult. Some find that it helps them concentrate better. Consult your doctor about all matters related to medication for ADD.

- Meditation or other soothing activities may also help adults with ADD slow down their minds and relax.

4

Cooperating with Co-Workers and Networking

"Maybe it would be better if we put [having ADD] out there. There are some people who could handle it well and assist you in getting the job done without judging you."

—CAITLIN, ATTORNEY

■ Offending Others Without Meaning To

Leaders who have ADD tend to be open to multiple points of view. They like working with a team and benefiting from what other people can bring to the table. This egalitarian approach also tends to be true of ADD adults as a whole. For example, Winona, a New York actress and filmmaker, loved working on a traveling theater tour of eight actors. She handled costumes while others did the scenery, and she describes that collaboration as the best environment in which she's ever worked.

In fact, although they often like the freedom afforded by working for themselves, people with ADD also generally enjoy the camaraderie and stimulation that come from working with colleagues. Sean, an independent business consultant, admits that "self-employment is difficult. I work better in a team. It's hard to be a lone ranger." Though he's been successful starting his own consulting business, he misses the collegiality of working in an office.

The fact that adults with ADD enjoy working with others makes it all the more painful that they may inconvenience, fluster, or annoy their co-workers with their different styles of working or learning. Angry responses from colleagues may take ADD adults aback because they don't always realize that their impulsivity, procrastination, perfectionism, or other tendencies can affect those around them.

Tom, a university director of development, says, "People with ADD are attacked by their peers because of the frustration they create, but they don't know why their behavior causes consequences. It creates paranoia, and you don't know why your peers are your enemies."

This chapter discusses some of the challenges and opportunities ADD adults experience working with others and provides insight into how they can reflect on their behavior and appreciate how it affects others and how the behavior of their co-workers affects them.

■ Open Mouth, Insert Foot

Vanessa, a New York City public school teacher, admits she has the tendency to blurt out things in meetings and interrupt her co-workers. To counter this impulse, she says, "I scribble during all the meeting to remember things, keep myself focused, and not interrupt. It helps me keep track of my ideas and not get bored." She also sometimes wears a rubber band on her wrist to remind her not to interrupt her colleagues. A simple snap against her skin is sufficient to keep her quiet.

Michelle, a social worker in Tennessee, says she "has had a few head-butts with people." After these run-ins, "I go to them and say 'excuse me I have an impulse problem.'" Sometimes, she finds that she's trying to defend herself for having done work that she was sure she completed but that she didn't actually do. "I've been so dead sure that I did something when I didn't, and I had to apologize for it," she says. When making her apologies, "I don't necessarily cite ADD because people see it as an excuse for being irresponsible. They don't care [that I have ADD] if they need something from me."

To counteract their tendency to blurt out things, coach Becca Gross suggests that ADD adults ask a buddy at work how what they said sounded at meetings. She advises her clients to ask, "Is what I said appropriate?" noting that adults with ADD often "feel like they're coming across as intimidating or overly aggressive." This type of feedback can help you be more reflective and to think before you speak.

Sometimes the impatience of ADD adults spills into anger and aggression. Brian, who works as a successful independent IT consultant, has always had difficulty with what he calls his "professionalism." He explains, "My behavior has been considered unconventional and not following protocol." In an earlier job in operations at a financial services firm, he had to place notices about different matters on the desks of brokers. One broker claimed that he never received a specific notice and taunted Brian about it for several minutes. "I reached through the glass partition dividing our offices and tried to choke him," Brian recalls. "My temper and ability to control myself are always an issue."

Brian decided to work as an independent contractor so he didn't have to deal with office politics. "I avoid politics and just show up and do the job," he says. If he runs into a difficult situation on the job, he takes a break and temporarily walks out of the office or calls someone on his cell phone to calm himself. Now, he describes his relationships with his clients as "usually good, occasionally confrontational." When he challenges his clients about something, "Some people can handle it and some can't," he says. "The last group I worked with told me to shut up, and we moved on. If people take it personally, it's a problem." He has found that he does better by choosing to work with people who can handle his confrontational nature.

■ Comparing Yourself to Others

Since they were children, many ADD adults have realized that they have to work harder than other people to achieve the same results. In school, they often had to struggle to complete their work and felt that their problems reflected an underlying deficit in intelligence—even though it didn't. As adults, they may still have to work longer hours, and they sometimes find it dispiriting to look at the seeming ease with which co-workers complete their work. Vanessa, for example, works longer hours than the other teachers in her school, and Zoe, the sales executive, has to work 24-7 to keep up with the demands of her high-powered job.

Ben, a computer usability engineer, has to continually remind himself that he's not like other people. "It helps to talk to people who understand me and what I've dealt with," he says. "I have to let go of the results and just do my work and not be too hard on myself." Ben used to drink to relieve the pressure he felt, but he has been sober for many years. He now relieves pressure by exercising and meditation, and these tools help him stay focused and calm.

Tom, a university director of development, realized early on that he shouldn't compare himself to others. He had difficulty learning to read in school, and he visited a learning specialist who told him that there was nothing evil in the way his brain worked. Now, he accepts occasional slip-ups and knows that he sometimes will miss an appointment. "I've taught myself not to hit the floor and to take [mistakes] in stride," he says. "I used to be aggressive about it. If it's going to happen, I try to learn from it."

▓ Perfectionism

Perfectionism often dogs ADD adults. Indeed, sometimes, the very things that make ADD adults exceptional workers can get them in trouble with their co-workers. Often, ADD workers want to continually redo projects until they are perfect while their colleagues are waiting for them to get the job done.

For example, Aaron, a lighting designer, has always enjoyed seeking out new ways of doing things, and this can slow down his projects. "I would add to my current load to make it more exciting, so I took on more than I could chew," he says. "If there were five different types of lighting in the living room, I would create a computer spreadsheet with formulas, while I could have easily done it with paper and pencil. I would make work for myself, and people got upset because I spent too much time." While this kind of planning helped Aaron in the long term, there were no immediate results from it, and, in his words, "most employers don't have the long run in mind."

Brian, an independent IT consultant, tends to get "bogged down in minutiae. Organization is not my strong point, so I have to force myself to prioritize," he says. "If I'm given priorities, that makes it easier. If I'm not, I create my own and question people to get their input." Although Brian works on a consulting basis and changes jobs every few months, he makes sure to identify the key stakeholders at each job and get their input. Asking them what's important and prioritizing the client's goals allows him to get beyond his tendency to obsess over the small details of an assignment.

Sometimes, ADD adults will become glued to their work as a means of controlling one aspect of their lives and ignoring more troubling, less predictable arenas of their lives. Margaret, a professor at a liberal arts college, says, "Before my husband and I knew about my anxiety and ADD, we called it 'work addiction.' I struggled with it, and we both said that if the problem was alcohol, we would say I shouldn't drink. With work, though, you can't say 'don't work.' You have to work, so the struggle is to manage the addiction." In her case, recognizing and treating her ADD and anxiety made it possible for her to manage her work addiction and achieve a greater sense of balance in her life. Her personal life benefited as a result. "I find interpersonal and family time and social activities more enjoyable than before," she says. "I used to be the prototypical wall flower—I would be scrunched up against the wall."

Howard, a lawyer, can't focus until he's under pressure, but that doesn't mean he's kicking back until deadline time. In fact, his whole work cycle is filled with anxiety. "I'm anxious enough that I don't completely relax when I'm not under the gun. I feel like I should be working all the time because I think I'm getting behind," he says. "But because I can't focus, I work inefficiently all the time and only efficiently in crunch times. Before I had my diagnosis, I thought of it as a character flaw, so I stayed at the office all the time to punish myself and impoverished all other areas of my life." Howard says he has "become perfectionistic out of fear that I have to compensate for other deficits." In the process, he has chosen to work a great deal of hours, to the detriment of other areas of his life.

◼ Getting Help from Co-Workers

Co-workers can be a great resource for ADD adults. Kind colleagues can help ADD adults with aspects of their work at which they may not be as strong, but not every ADD worker feels comfortable asking for a helping hand.

"If you have very low self-esteem," says Eve, an architect and fashion designer, "you may not learn from others. I couldn't allow myself to learn information. If you felt worthy of learning, you would." Her low sense of self-worth often prevents Eve from asking others for assistance or letting them know that she doesn't understand how to do something.

Other adults with ADD have found that they can make requests of helpful colleagues. Michelle, a social worker, asks her co-workers to help her with time sheets. "The other day I was trying to do a time sheet, and I told a nurturing lady at work that I had ADD, and she helped me," Michelle explains. Katherine, the lawyer for people with disabilities, has her co-workers proofread everything she writes.

Rachel, a psychiatrist, now asks her colleagues to help her read schedules because of a disastrous mistake that she made as a medical resident. She was supposed to be on call one night, but she looked at the schedule and didn't read it correctly and erroneously left the hospital. "For a resident to blow off a night of call is a disaster. I could have lost my job and career," she says. Fortunately, her colleagues reacted compassionately, and instead of being fired, she was tested in her clinic for ADD. "They told me I was the most clear-cut case they'd ever seen," Rachel recalls.

"I still look at things like lists and pieces of paper and don't see what's on the page," she says. "I don't have a reading disorder—I don't *see* the words." Now, Rachel asks her medical colleagues to help her read her work schedule. "At lunch, they give your call schedule, and my peers are willing to see if I'm on call," she says. "I ask a different person every week to check for me, and they're very supportive." She carries a laptop with her wherever she goes in her ward so she can immediately enter her tasks and appointments on her to-do list. She tells the attending physicians that she has ADD to explain why she totes her laptop around with her.

Caitlin, a Philadelphia lawyer, doesn't ask for a great deal of help from her co-workers but wonders if perhaps she should. "There are some people who could handle it well and assist you in getting the job done without judging you," she says. Caitlin says the bookkeeper at her law firm knows she has ADD and understands how to help her. "If I had brought it out, maybe more people could have helped me," she believes. While Caitlin doesn't think there's much use in telling the managing partner of her firm she has ADD because "he already knows me and has made judgments," she thinks it may be helpful to let more of the administrative staff know about her ADD and the kinds of assistance she needs as a result.

Zoe, a sales executive, often has a hard time concentrating during meetings and catching everything that is said. "If others talk about a meeting, it's clear that they understood it much more deeply than I did," she says. Asking others to keep notes during a meeting or talking about meetings with helpful co-workers may enable ADD adults to keep better track of what goes on.

■ Successful Networking

Networking is the process that puts all your talents and skills into play. It's what gets you out into the world and face-to-face with potential customers, clients, and employers. It's particularly important in today's volatile work environment, in which no job lasts forever. You never know when you'll be pounding the pavement looking for a new position. If you keep your networks in good shape by attending to them while you have a job, you'll be in a better position when things change.

However, many ADD adults report that they don't have the time or the inclination to routinely and systematically make contacts and keep them in order. Most of the adults I interviewed said they don't do any networking at all or only use low-impact means such as e-mail to contact colleagues and business associates. Successful ADD adults tend to put so much time into their jobs that they don't have the energy to dedicate to networking, but some tips can help you keep your networks in good shape in ways that take minimal amounts of time.

Connect with One Person at a Time

Adults with ADD often find that they don't have the concentration to attend networking events. To counteract this, ADD coach Linda Anderson suggests that some ADD adults take their medica-

How to Enlist Help

The inability of many adults to ask for help means that their great ideas may never come to fruition, and the world may be poorer as a result. For example, Stacey, a physical education teacher for special education kids, tried to develop a TV talk show for children several years ago. She had contacts in the field and was well on her way. The project went off the rails, however, when she needed help to push it forward but didn't know how to get it. "I've always done everything myself and don't know how to ask for help," she says. "I'm so independent. I learned to be that way as a child."

But because ADD adults tend to have so much to offer, including an all-too-rare sense of humor and fun, they may find colleagues more receptive to their requests for help than they might expect. Stacey, for example, brings "squishies" to boring meetings to liven up the atmosphere, and her colleagues have been very appreciative of these gestures. Perhaps if adults with ADD begin to appreciate how much they add to their work environments and take a realistic inventory of their very real strengths, if necessary with the help of a coach, counselor, or friend, they will feel more justified in asking for help. We will all benefit as a result because their great ideas will be able to blossom.

tions right before a party or networking event so they can better concentrate.

Anderson says that while the majority of ADD adults have no problem making connections and are quite lively and social, "for many 'ADDers,' the relationship piece is a distraction, and they forget to have relationships. They miss things in conversation, and some hate parties. It's a negative experience to go into a situation and realize you're missing cues." She suggests that such clients concentrate on speaking to one person who does what the client wants to do, instead of working to connect with ten people at once. She also tells clients to focus on attending one event rather than many. "I narrow it down for them to the doable," she says.

Some career seekers are tempted to attend multiple parties and exhaust themselves meeting a ton of contacts, but the quality of the contacts outweighs the quantity. This means it's often profitable to contact the person who's likely to be the most helpful to you first. This person usually is a friend of a friend or has some personal connection to you that will make him or her more likely to dedicate time to you. In addition, this person is very closely connected to the work you want to do or to potential customers. Working down your list of contacts, from the most important to the least, will enable you to structure your networking in a manageable, productive way.

Network with Your Friends

Lois, an artist who looks for new clients, has found that she does better at networking that involves issues and people she cares about. "Value-based networking compels me to engage. It's not just schmoozing, but being part of a community," she says. "It helps if you're interested in the event or cause."

Becca Gross, an ADD coach, tells her clients to "trust what

works for you in terms of people you connect with. If you relate to people who are entrepreneurs, be open to that."

Caroline, a computer instructor and freelance consultant and coach, recruited clients by passing out her business cards at an ADD support group. Support groups can be a great way for adults with ADD to network. She also finds that she's more likely to attend a networking event if she goes with another person, such as her sister. Caroline attended a networking cocktail party several months ago just to "check it out." She says she'll return to press the flesh. "Now that I've been once, it will be easy to go back and hand out my card," she says.

Zoe, a $200,000-a-year sales executive, suggests that an ADD support group for professionals might be a great vehicle for people at the top echelons of their industries to connect in a comfortable, meaningful way. She says that given her 24-7 work life, she doesn't have that much time to read books about ADD. Zoe thinks an ADD support network for high-level executives might provide her with the tools she needs and might help her see how ADD benefits her work and how she can capitalize on her inherent strengths.

Use Your Creativity and Energy

ADD adults may turn networking events and marketing vehicles in their favor by capitalizing on their creativity. Sara, a singer/songwriter in Texas, set her band apart from the pack by producing an eye-catching newsletter. While other bands generally staple flyers to telephone poles, Sara created a cleverly written newsletter with advertisements that paid for the mailing and printing costs. "It helped bring people to the act, and clubs and recording companies picked up on it," she says.

The newsletter Sara created featured pictures of the band in the studio with the producer and photos of their friends playing with major acts. Sara's dog was the pictured editor of the publication, and there were photos of the dog smelling new CDs in an attempt to evaluate them. The pooch was also pictured attending meetings. The circulation of the newsletter reached 5,000—an impressive number for a local band.

ADD adults aren't often held back by convention, and this can allow them to knock on doors and use their energy to make new contacts. For example, when Tom, now the director of development at a graduate school, received his current job, he had never worked in development before. He decided spontaneously to drop in on the head of development at a prestigious graduate school—even though he'd never met this man before. Now, this other development director has become Tom's mentor and has given him excellent advice and strategies that Tom credits with helping him close many multimillion-dollar gifts.

When Will, an A&R person and record producer, took his first artist on the road for a month-long cross-country tour, he found it difficult to be organized. "The whole crew of guys was looking to me to set up hotels and asking me 'When is sound check?'" he recalls. Will at first found himself struggling with knowing how to handle the tour and told himself, "You gotta get on your game." He decided to reach out to other tour managers and make them his friends. "I called them at every stop," he says. "They opened up their books and said, 'this is how you do it.'" He used his considerable charm to get help from others who knew the ropes.

How to Organize Your Networking

While many ADD adults are the life of the party, they may not profit from networking due to their disorganization. Business and ADD coach Bonnie Mincu says ADD adults need "more structure in getting it together to network and follow through. An 'ADDer' may need to think where he or she will put business cards and how to structure the follow up and get intentional strategy out of networking." She suggests to clients that they write a note on the back of business cards they collect at networking events to jog their memory about the people they meet.

ADD coach Becca Gross suggests that clients who have a sense of social impairment should plan what they might talk about before they attend events. "Understand that if you don't know what to say to someone new, you're not bad at dealing with people but you just get boggled." She advises clients to script what they're going to say before the event and to have a few conversational items ready for small talk.

Using computer software can help you keep your contacts in good order and make them accessible for future reference. Caroline, the computer consultant and coach, keeps her contacts organized on her computer using software such as Excel or Access. Lois, the artist, has kept cards for each client, which she updates with each new contact. She hasn't done this consistently, however, which causes her problems in tracking her clientele.

Preparing for events helps ADD adults get more out of them. Katherine, a lawyer working in the area of disabilities, serves on several committees in the legal community. She finds that she can participate to a greater extent in the meetings if she prepares for them. "I have to read things beforehand—I can't read in the meeting like other people. If I participate, I feel more a part of it."

Networking to Find a New Job

ADD coach Jennifer Koretsky works with many clients who are in between jobs. "That can be a problem," she says. "When people are in between jobs and are networking to find a job, there's procrastination. It's more about fear and lack of a plan, so a plan helps."

She tells clients not to hold it against themselves if they're not work-ing from 9 to 5 every day to find a new job. "Even if you only send out résumés for one hour a day, that's more than you had done yes-terday," she tells them.

Keep in mind that if you are self-employed, you may need to network continuously and that former co-workers and contacts are your best means of finding new work. You can't just let your con-tacts lie dormant but have to check in with them on a regular basis; they are like a garden that needs continual tending to prosper. For example, Brian, an independent IT consultant, networks through people he's met on jobs in the past, including vendors and former colleagues on projects. "I recently sent a vendor I'd worked with on a project an e-mail looking for a job, and the vendor knew a person who needed someone," Brian explains. "I also know a lot of con-sultants and shoot them e-mail or send along e-mails I receive from recruiters." Using e-mail and phone calls to contacts, Brian keeps up with his informal network of friends and colleagues. He only rarely attends professional networking events because he finds that they're not held at convenient times. Instead, cultivating his rich personal network allows him to successfully move from one consulting job to another every few months.

Wilma Fellman, a career and life-planning coach who has worked extensively with ADD adults, says that in finding a new job, "Networking is the key—the more people you talk to about every-thing, the more firsthand information you're going to get." She sug-gests that "once you come up with a few ideas you're toying with, speak to a few people in the area. ADD people can be gregarious as long as they have done their homework and know that this is a field that will be good for them."

Fellman helps her clients produce a script to use in the interview, and she suggests having a list of questions, not simply saying "tell me about this field." She says, "ADD adults need to know about the field in terms of their match [with it]. They should probe for things based on how ADD affects them without coming out and saying they have ADD." (Remember that by law, employers can't ask whether you have a disability such as ADD during the hiring process itself.)

Fellman suggests that people ask questions such as "Could you describe a typical day?" and advises her clients to "try it on mentally for size in terms of the task and the environment. Many ADD adults are affected by the environment, including lighting, sound, texture, and the buzzing of fluorescent lights." She tells her clients to do their networking in person so they can get the whole picture of what a job involves and what it's like to work in that particular environment.

She also advises her clients to ask people who are in a prospective field what the drawbacks of their job are but notes that "for an ADD person, a drawback might actually be a plus. For example, someone might say a drawback is that you have to do six things at once, but the person with ADD may need to do many things at once or they're not stimulated." Fellman thinks it's optimal if people observe someone in a job they're interested in. "'Firsthandness' is really good for someone with ADD," she says. "We make assumptions about what people do and what their day feels like, and we don't have a realistic picture of what it's like."

Fellman notes that when she started practicing twenty-one years ago, there was a big difference between ADD and non-ADD résumés because "the ADD person had a sketchy résumé, but that's not true today because there's been a shift in the general population from staying in one job to most people having two or more careers in their life and countless jobs," she says. "When you get a résumé from someone who has been at several places, it's not looked at askance. In the future, fewer and fewer people, less than the majority, will have forty-hour weeks in one place. Most people will have a portfolio career that involves twenty hours in one place, twenty hours in another because it's wise to hedge your bets against unemployment. The whole emphasis has helped the ADD individual not look so unusual."

Going Back to School

Many ADD adults actually do better in post-college work than they do in high school or college because graduate study allows them to focus on their passions while working in a less rigid way. For example, Howard, a lawyer who received bachelor's, master's, and law degrees all from Ivy League universities, says that while he did fine at college, graduate school "allowed me to take off because I didn't have deadlines. I could take time to make my papers good enough so my anxiety would drop." He says, "Law school is not so bad for people with ADD because you don't have a dissertation to write. You read cases in small bites, and there's one exam per semester you cram for." Although Howard did well in law school, he had the frustrating experience of being recognized as smart in class but didn't do as well on exams. "Law school favors grinders," he says.

Career and life planning counselor Wilma Fellman says that when ADD adults are considering returning to school, "the cardinal rule is that before they take classes, they should go through the data collection career development process. They should have their goal firmly set in mind before taking classes. If you know your goal will be right for you, this confirmation will help you feel calm and focused. ADD adults have already encountered numerous failings, and all that begins to come into their focus more than reaching their goal. If they're right for what they're going after and they know that because of hard data, school will be a fabulous experience."

• ● •CHAPTER HIGHLIGHTS• ● •

■ ADD adults often enjoy working with their co-workers, so it can come as a painful shock that their disorganization and poor time-management skills may be causing their colleagues annoyance. Not understanding how their work styles affect others can result in ADD adults feeling paranoid or confused.

■ Some adults with ADD suffer from impulsivity and may need conscious strategies to prevent them from interrupting colleagues or offering hurtful advice. Coaches suggest enlisting a helpful friend to tell you when you've said the wrong thing at a meeting or to a co-worker. ADD adults may also do better working with people who don't take their blunt comments to heart.

■ Adults with ADD often have to work harder and longer than others. This can cause a great deal of stress, so it may be helpful to talk about it with others who are in your same boat or to use stress-reduction techniques such as exercise and meditation.

■ As a result of their feelings of low self-worth and their desire to make things perfect, ADD workers can get bogged down in one stage of a project, much to the consternation of fellow workers. They are helped by recognizing this tendency and moving forward. Otherwise, they may become workaholics and their personal lives may suffer.

■ Some ADD adults have been helped by reaching out for help to trusted co-workers to get assistance with tasks that they aren't good at. While it is difficult for some ADD workers to ask for help, they may not be able to bring their great ideas to fruition if they don't do so. It may help if they understand how much they bring to the workplace and that their co-workers value their input and contribution to the workplace. After all, ADD workers often add a great deal of fun and spontaneity to what would otherwise be a very dull environment.

■ Successful ADD adults tend to put so much time into their jobs that they don't have the energy to dedicate to networking, but some tips can help you maintain and develop your networks in ways that take minimal amounts of time.

■ When networking, concentrate on speaking with one person who does what you want to do, instead of working to connect with ten people at once. Choose people who have the closest personal and work connections to you first, and then contact less productive contacts.

■ Networking with people and issues you care about may make the process easier and more natural for you.

■ Take time to prepare for events and script out small talk if you find this is a problem for you.

■ After a networking event, take time to organize your contacts, perhaps using database software programs, and plan how you will follow up with people you meet.

■ Use your boundless energy and creativity to make the networking process work for you and give yourself an advantage.

■ While networking for a new job, collect as much data as you can and ask specifically about things you think will be a challenge, without necessarily mentioning that you have ADD.

■ A résumé with a lot of career changes and shifts may not necessarily scare off employers. Although this type of résumé used to be characteristic of ADD adults and not the general population, a change in employment practices has made it more common for all adults to profit from career shifts and to have eclectic work histories.

- Be sure your advanced education fits in with your goals; if you have clear goals and know your education will help you reach them, you're more likely to have a fruitful, enjoyable experience when you return to school.

5

Maximizing Your Strengths

"I'm just very me and very funny—open, no bull, no agenda. I say what I feel, and the level of communication that I have and inspire in others is so much more real than what they usually find. People who aren't threatened by it really like it."

—ZOE, SALES EXECUTIVE

Realizing That ADD Can Help You

ADD adults have spent a lot of their lives hearing that they don't measure up at school and work. They may not even realize that they have very real strengths that are a direct result of what is referred to as their "disorder." While each person has his or her particular strengths, which are a by-product of upbringing, personality, and inborn skills, there are some common gifts among ADD adults. These are easy for the attentive outsider to see.

Many of the ADD adults I interviewed for this book are incredibly creative. In the course of our one- or two-hour conversation, they would offhandedly mention innovative ideas they had for new children's product lines or give me great ideas about books I could write. But when I asked them how having ADD had helped their work in any way, they often drew a blank. They didn't realize how novel their ideas were or that not everyone could found successful independent businesses, as many of them had.

"How can ADD possibly help me?" many of them responded, especially if they were in the throes of struggling with the disorder.

However, some of the adults who had come to terms with their disorder and who had worked to manage its sticky issues believed that having ADD had helped them. They thought their successes at work would not have been possible if they had a brain that worked differently. David Neeleman, the CEO of JetBlue Airways, even thinks that his success is a *direct result* of having ADD. In a June 1, 2003, *New York Times* article, Neeleman explained why he'd never taken medication for his ADD by saying, "I'm afraid I'll take it once, blow a circuit, and then I'd be like the rest of you." David Neeleman has made his airline work differently than the rest of the industry, and because of that difference, JetBlue is prospering in the worst climate for the aviation industry in decades.

It takes many ADD adults a while to get to the place where they appreciate their particular mix of talents. Linda Anderson, an ADD coach based in Pennsylvania, tells the story of one of her clients who had won the Pulitzer prize. When Anderson, then working as a professional organizer, went to her client's penthouse, the client would sit on the floor in tears and ask why she couldn't organize her house like everyone else. "People get stuck in places where they feel insufficient," Anderson says.

Many adults with ADD have to overcome a lifetime of hearing that they're insufficient and dive deep to find their talents that lie beneath the surface. Often, it's just that the "window dressing" is missing—for example, some students are poor spellers, but they have wonderful, creative ideas that lie obscured beneath their poorly spelled words. Similarly, many ADD adults are rough-cut gems, and they can shine if they are shaped in the right ways. They may get tripped up early in their careers at entry-level jobs that require attention to detail and obedience to structure, which doesn't let their higher-order thinking and creativity come to the fore.

Rosa, an aspiring Hollywood screenwriter, is the perfect example. She always considered herself a horrible writer and struggled through high school in Puerto Rico, where she produced papers that were returned to her covered with critical red marks. One of her college professors told her she was the worst writer he'd ever come across. Somehow, Rosa had enough confidence to pursue a graduate degree in dramatic writing at a prestigious U.S. film school. She hadn't even realized that she could write until she came across a trunk full of letters and free-form journals in her attic. While her thoughts often meander on the page, it is precisely Rosa's inability to stick to one strict plot line that gives her writing its creative power. Her innovative screenplays mix genres, such as thrillers and love stories, and she had an independent script accepted into the finals at the Sundance Film Festival. During all those years when she was crying over papers marked with red ink, Rosa never realized that her prodigious talents were waiting to blossom. There are many ADD adults like Rosa whose inability to stick to the script of life obscures their underlying creative genius.

■ Recognizing Your Strengths

Like Rosa, the screenwriter who came upon a trunk full of letters in her attic that caused her to realize she had a real talent for creative writing, you may come to identify some of your talents by searching deep in your past. It may help to hear the stories of other ADD adults. Reading this chapter may enable you to see some of the qualities you thought were total detriments in a new, more positive light. Maybe you never realized that your ADD brain in the right context was not only a disadvantage but actually a real advantage that sets you apart from everyone else.

If you have trouble recognizing your strengths, you may want to ask a friend or a supportive co-worker what he or she sees as your special talents. If negative self-talk still gets in the way of hearing positive feedback from friends and co-workers, you may want to consider working with a therapist.

In fact, you may have too many talents to focus on just one. ADD adults often are talented in many arenas, and they want to engage all their interests at once. Massachusetts ADD coach Becca Gross says her clients tend to have "passion that goes all over the place, but they often don't get the positives of ADD at first." In fact, many of her clients can't decide what to do because "they love all these things." She says that her clients' "need for change, high level of stimulation, and high level of risk and intensity are really neat things, so I help people see what the good side of it is and how to apply it. It may mean a change in your lifestyle, job, or in how you see yourself."

Your strengths are not only a function of your innate talents but also the environment in which you use them. Sometimes, you may simply be in the wrong environment or job to make them shine. For example, Katherine, the disabilities lawyer, made a horrible paralegal but is very successful as an attorney because she delegates some of the detail-oriented work that she can't handle and is able to operate on a more conceptual level on which she excels. In Chapter 6, we will discuss the elements of a workplace that is amenable to ADD and that capitalizes on ADD talents.

If you feel that you have talents but that they're not being used or recognized in your current work situation, you may want to assess, with the help of a career counselor, how to reach a place that is more conducive to your abilities and work style.

Let's look at the strengths of adults with ADD and see how they have worked to great advantage in their careers.

■ Energy and Risk-Taking

James, a lawyer now in his mid-fifties, didn't know he had ADD until a few years ago, but his characteristic ADD qualities, including his lack of inhibition and his willingness to take risks, have helped him throughout his career. When he was in graduate school, he met Mayor Lindsay of New York City at the urinals in the men's room during a conference. Taking full advantage of the situation, James introduced himself to the mayor—a bold move that a more reserved person may not have made.

His daring paid off handsomely. A year later, James got an internship at the mayor's office through his graduate school. When James went to meet Mayor Lindsay for a clearance interview, the mayor remembered him and wholeheartedly agreed that James should work in his office. The mayor liked James's outgoing nature and his initiative and thought these qualities would help the intern in his work.

Throughout his career, James's lack of inhibition has helped him ask for what he needs—and get it. In law school, he became an advocate for himself and persuaded the administration to let him use a typewriter for in-class exams because he found he was only producing one-third of what other students did on written tests. What someone might cast as a problematic degree of impulsivity or an impolitic tendency to tell the truth and ask for what he needs might also, in James's case, be considered a healthy directness that brings about quick, definite results. The lack of inhibition that often accompanies ADD can be a boon in the competitive work world.

■ Pioneering New Movements

Jake, a former lawyer, believes that his greatest accomplishment to date has been harnessing his intense passion for bicycling that he first developed in college. As cycling became more and more central to his life, he initiated a lobby in his state that was remarkably successful in advocating for cyclists.

"I still don't know how I pulled it off," the lawyer says, "but I sustained my activity in the lobby because people looked to me." He eventually became the adviser to his state's governor on bicycling matters. Rather than feeling that his interests are too diffuse, Jake credits his large number of interests in attracting his wife to him.

Jake's passion to create something new arose from his intense energy and passion for cycling, and he gained speed by feeding off this energy. The new movement gained its own momentum over time— much like a bike going downhill—and Jake was remarkably successful in cycling his passion into a lobby that wound up helping other cyclists across his state. Jake's efforts built off his passion for biking, as well as his deep-felt desire to make his state a better place to live. ADD adults often have a great deal of passion that can overcome whatever obstacles lie in their path.

■ Compassion and Empathy

The daughter of a public-school teacher, Stacey was never a good student—much to her mother's chagrin. In a misguided attempt to help their daughter improve her grades, her parents prohibited her from watching television for an entire year, but Stacey couldn't kick the TV habit. For years, Stacey put herself down for being addicted to television, until she realized that watching television gave her the down time that's necessary to keep herself going.

Her unhappy childhood spiraled into a strange double existence in which she worked successfully in the camping industry and, in her private life, became addicted to using cocaine and crack. She credits the love she's gotten from kids over the years with saving her life and getting her off drugs. "The kids always accepted me for who I was," she explains. She was later diagnosed with ADD, and her life started to turn around. Now, she works as a physical education teacher for kids with special needs and as a freelance consultant to help parents find camps that are right for their kids.

"I totally identify with children," she says. "I understand having a hidden disability and the pain of children when people don't respect them. My work is about helping kids feel good about themselves." Her love for children has kept Stacey going through long days at school and long nights working as a camp consultant. "I'm very well respected by the parents I work with because I understand kids. Kids love me, and I love them and know the pain they're in— it's mutual. I get the self-esteem I never got growing up from my relationships with kids."

Stacey is now open at work about having ADD, and when she's at a meeting, she'll bring toys like "squishies" for people to play with, a gesture that her co-workers find endearing and helpful. "It turned out over time that a lot of people identify with having ADD but don't talk about it," she says. "I'm light about it and just say, 'there goes my ADD.'"

Vanessa, New York City public school teacher, also brings an immense amount of compassion and understanding to her work. She can recognize the kids in her class with ADD—not just the hyperactive "fidget monsters" but also the inattentive, daydreamy kids— and she knows how to help them using the hard-won knowledge that comes from her own struggles as a kid. She gives the hyperactive students rubber bands to play with unobtrusively during lessons, and she credits this technique with managing their symptoms in a way that helps them and her. She can orchestrate the seating of her children in the classroom to her own and her students' advantages. She puts the hyperactive kids in the periphery of her vision so they don't disturb her, while she places the daydreamers front and center so they're forced to pay better attention.

Vanessa believes that educators tend to have negative associations with ADD students because they've been unsuccessful working with them, particularly the hyperactive children. She's able to succeed with these children "because I don't personalize their problems. I know what they're thinking, and I'm able to identify with kids with problems." While speaking to me in a Brooklyn, New York, bookstore about the number of children who were labeled "at risk" whom she's been able to help, Vanessa's eyes well up with tears and she reaches for a tissue from her book bag. Just then, she catches sight of a toddler whose scarf has fallen on the floor. Vanessa runs across the bookstore's café and whisks the scarf off the floor and returns it to the child's mother. "My work is about love," she says when she returns to our table. "By treating my ADD, I'm better able to love children."

Margaret, a professor at a prestigious Midwestern liberal arts college, has been better able to work with students with learning disabilities since she was diagnosed with ADD herself at age forty-five. "I first heard the phrase 'ADD' when a student had failed her comprehensive exam for a second time, and I laughed out loud," she recalls. "How could I have been so cruel?"

Margaret is becoming a better teacher because "I understand things about different learning styles that I didn't have a clue about before. This semester, I have several dyslexic and ADD students. What's interesting is that I can tell from my interactions with them that the kids have been burned a lot in the past." She has learned to assign her first-year students work that helps them make sense of the reading. This year, she told them that for each reading assignment, they could write a paragraph, look up definitions for words they didn't know, draw a map, or search for images on the Web to send to her with captions. She's been amazed by the number of kids who draw maps—about a quarter of them—and she now realizes that many of her students learn better through visual rather than written representations of information. Her own awakening to her ADD has allowed Margaret to be a more compassionate, open educator.

The more Rachel, a psychiatrist who has been diagnosed with ADD, accepts herself with all her problems, the more she says she is able to remember to see her patients as well-rounded, nuanced people with problems—not merely as diagnoses. "It's difficult to be seen as sick," she says. "I see my own pluses and minuses and those of others." She is a different kind of psychiatrist precisely because she has endured her own battles with ADD and what it means to have a "disorder." Like Rachel, adults with ADD know firsthand the pain of being misunderstood, and they have a greater well of understanding and acceptance as a result.

■ Helping Others Have Fun: Dancing on the Desk!

Zoe is one of the most vibrant people I've ever spoken with. After an hour-long whirlwind telephone conversation, during which she walked around Manhattan mailing packages and picking up her dry cleaning while talking on her cell phone, I felt exhausted but elated. I was sorry to put down the phone—Zoe is someone I'd like to call every day for a pick-me-up that's far more potent than a double latte. Her infectious energy has driven her to be a $200,000-per-year sales executive. And yet she feels dogged by the complaints of some of her more buttoned-down co-workers that's she's just too aggressive, too wild, and not exactly "corporate."

Luckily, that's not how her clients feel. Her client at IBM chose to work with her because she's fun, and in the often dry world of business, Zoe stands out. In her previous position, people loved working with her because she got up on her desk and started singing and tap-dancing. Even the staid researchers at her old company told her she was the most motivating person in the firm. "I don't act all corporate and protocol-ish," she says. "I'm just very me and very funny—open, no bull, no agenda. I say what I feel, and the level of communication that I have and inspire in others is so much more real than what they usually find. People who aren't threatened by it really like it."

Adults with ADD understand their own restless natures, and they know how to keep others interested. They are aware that even people without ADD don't appreciate being bored, and they can offer others high energy and creativity that hold their interest. April, the sales consultant in Texas, knows people can easily grow bored in dull corporate training sessions, and her own restlessness and energy make her an exceedingly dynamic presenter. When she consults to Fortune 500 companies, she doesn't compose a fifty-page curriculum binder that would fill managers with dread and immediately sap their energy. Instead, she gives them one page with the meeting agenda, and she infuses her presentations with high energy and makes them entertaining. "I don't read to clients, and they love it," she says. She used to beat herself up for not being able to produce large binders for meetings, but now she realizes that in her seminars, "my clients say they learn a lot more."

■ Maximizing Your Creativity

The brain of the ADD adult tends to allow in a greater number of unfiltered stimuli, and this rush of ideas can give people a heightened sense of what's possible. Because ADD allows for unfettered access to the total universe of ideas, many adults with this condition have great powers of creativity and invention. In fact, the creative process of ADD adults is difficult for non-ADD people to understand, and the manner in which these adults arrive at new ideas involves intuitive, nonlinear leaps that may seem unfathomable to others.

A good example of this kind of imaginative, leap-taking thinker is Jennifer Stewart, an actress who has for almost twenty years played the Statue of Liberty through her performances at various kinds of events as Living Liberty. In the mid-1980s, she wanted to design a Statue of Liberty costume to enter a national contest. Her desire to enter the contest was sparked by a comment made by a schizophrenic man she had been working with in art therapy the year before. He told her that she looked like Lady Liberty, and his comment lingered in her mind and later inspired her to enter the contest. The only problem was that Jennifer lived in Iowa and couldn't find an accurate photograph of the Statue of Liberty. All the pictures in magazines in the local library looked too blue. When her husband took an oxidized penny out of his pocket during lunch at a diner, she seized it. Her incredible visual strength made her realize that the oxidized penny was exactly the color she was looking for to make her Liberty costume.

Later, Jennifer got stuck thinking about how to make Liberty's crown and went to do her laundry. She looked at her laundry basket, and immediately her mind said "Use this!" Almost twenty years later, she still uses that crown. She explains her preternatural creativity this way: "In my brain, the circuit thing gets bypassed. Information gets spliced into new avenues."

Jennifer Stewart happens to have a particularly acute visual sense and has put it to colorful use, but ADD adults can bring their heightened sense of the possible to whatever area they work in. David Neeleman, CEO of JetBlue Airways, broke the barriers of what was possible in the aviation industry. No one thought an airline run out of JFK Airport in New York City could be profitable, or that you could have leather seats in coach. Neeleman was able to see that it was possible and then to prove it to the entire world.

■ Hyperfocusing and Multitasking

Many ADD adults recognize that their tendency to get into a groove and keep going in a task without loss of focus can be an advantage. It's interesting that many adults without ADD believe the disorder is one of wholesale broken or fragmented concentration, and they don't realize that ADD adults can have bursts of greater levels of focus than most other people. They often resist shifting their attention, and this can make them very productive for long stretches that would tire others out.

The term for this ability to concentrate on the task at hand and to narrow one's attention to the task while blocking out the rest of the world, even physical discomforts, is "hyperfocusing." ADD adults can use their amazing ability to focus and narrow their concentration in many ways. April, the sales consultant, can keep going in her office for hours on work that interests her without being distracted, while Jennifer Stewart, the actress who plays Living Liberty, found she could work endlessly on constructing her Lady Liberty costume without noticing her physical discomfort.

Caitlin, the Philadelphia lawyer, can focus on a case for a long time, a tendency that she thinks at times can be a disadvantage. "I can lock into something and can't make my mind think of something else," she says. "But I'm expected to keep a number of cases afloat and to change cases midstream."

ADD adults can also broaden their attention to focus on many stimuli at the same time. Many of the people I interviewed for this book could speak to me in a busy café while paying attention to what was going on at every other table and listening to the music playing in the background. I was shocked when one woman, who had spoken to me seamlessly for an hour, recalled almost every song that had been playing in a loud coffee house during our interview. If I had shifted my attention to the sound track, I wouldn't have been able to pay attention to the interview, but this woman could answer my questions, listen to the background music, and watch the passersby at the same time. It's almost as if her attention was more elastic and expansive, while mine was rigid and limited.

The ability of many ADD adults to focus simultaneously on many streams of sensory input boggles the mind of someone without ADD. For example, Sara, a singer/songwriter in Texas, can have many antennae up at the same time. In her work as a director of live shows, "I can wear a headset and have the spotlight operator speaking to me in one ear saying he can't find the target, while the guy in my other ear is asking 'Where's the drummer who has to go on next?' This would make most people completely freak out, but I remain calm and can switch between them," she says.

This ability to attend to many stimuli simultaneously goes beyond what is called "multitasking" in its level of complexity and difficulty, but it's a useful metaphor. Many of us can multitask to some degree—we can write an e-mail while listening to the radio, for example—but if the stimuli get to be too much, we start to break down and need to turn off the radio. Often, the opposite is true for adults with ADD. They sometimes *need* many streams of stimuli to keep going and stay focused, and successful adults with ADD tend to engage their minds by involving themselves in many things at once and by working at jobs that involve constant changes in their tasks.

For example, Jeff, the computer salesman, chose a job for which he has to change tacks many times during the day precisely because this kind of variation engages his attention. He likes working on one deal and then having to switch to a new promising customer opportunity without warning; his attentions can turn on a dime.

This embrace of spontaneity can be a real boon in the world of sports. Scott Eyre, the San Francisco Giants' relief pitcher, can get ready to face a hitter while speaking to a fan who's sitting right behind him in the stadium. As a left-handed "short reliever," he's often put in the game suddenly to face a left-handed hitter. "I'm put in the game and don't have time to think about it before it's done," he says. He works well with this kind of constantly changing schedule. When he was a starting pitcher, he would "continue to think about things on the mound" during his many off days. As a reliever, he has to be in the game every day, and this kind of flexible, spontaneous play suits him better.

Even sedentary jobs like law can be tailored to make good use of the ADD adult's tendency to embrace activity and restlessness. Katherine, the disabilities lawyer, designed her job so she could handle many tasks at once—including advocating for children, teaching, and doing outreach activities in the community. The diversity of her daily tasks and the opportunity they provide her to receive multiple stimuli help keep her motivated and interested in her work. Rather than enervate her, they energize her.

ADD adults are often uniquely suited for jobs that require constant shifts in attention and extreme degrees of invention and spontaneity. Winona, an actress and filmmaker, likes flying by the seat of her pants. She works at trade shows and can jump right into them and very quickly absorb the information about the products she's selling and learn her script in a matter of minutes. It's not only that she doesn't get frazzled, but also that she truly enjoys this kind of rapid learning and thrives in this kind of environment. Constant change feeds her mind, and she says the perfect job for her was being an actress on the theater tour she took to high schools across the country a few years ago. The combination of performing the same play every day in a different place provided the perfect degree of variability for her. On the other hand, she finds that she can't follow set scripts with carefully timed cues and stays away from this kind of scripted work.

Again, how we look at these kinds of traits is a matter of semantics and coloring. What might be called "flighty" or "impulsive" can also be thought of as "adaptable" and as being a "quick learner." In our ever-shifting world, these qualities can be a great asset in the right workplace.

▪ Determination

Adults with ADD are used to seeing non-ADD schoolmates and co-workers accomplish more in less time, and they are also used to having to work extra hours to get the job done. By definition, ADD adults know what it means to work hard. Effortless achievement has not by and large been their fate, and their victories are, therefore, harder won and require greater degrees of perseverance.

When Zoe, the successful sales executive, is stressed about having a lot on her plate, she responds by working more. "I work harder if I'm stressed," she says. "It's hard for me to put my work down. I want to fix it, even though I know intellectually that you're supposed to put it down." She generally works all weekend and until midnight on the weekdays. She clocks twelve-hour days on Sundays and about seventy-five hours during a typical week. When she falls asleep, it's often on top of her laptop in bed.

Michelle, a licensed clinical social worker in Tennessee, believes that having ADD has helped make her a more diligent worker. "I don't take for granted that something will get done," she says. "I'm more conscientious because I acknowledge that work takes me longer. I wind up being the tortoise who beats the hare because I have the tenacity to get the job done." Michelle's boss knows that when she gives her work, Michelle will be compulsive about getting it done, and her boss prizes Michelle's dependability.

Brian, an independent IT consultant, thinks his work ethic is stronger than that of most people in his field. "I will work until 11 P.M. and not complain," he says. "If I decide to do something, I will give a monumental effort until it's done—it can be damaging to personal relationships." Brian spent ten years studying for his undergraduate degree while working full-time, but at graduation, he still didn't feel happy. His only thought was "What now?"

The hard-working tendencies of ADD adults arise because they have been used to having to labor extra hours and give monumental effort, and they've gotten into the groove of expecting to have to make this kind of commitment. While a blessing to their bosses, this type of never-ending work schedule can start to wear on those who maintain it. Zoe, now in her mid-forties, never had a honeymoon because she didn't have time for it due to her overbooked work schedule. She says her long hours are starting to wear her out, but she still enjoys being an overachiever. When her boss recently told her that her sales target for the year was $2 million—already a formidable goal—her first reaction was to say, "Bull—it's $4 million!"

Assessing and Fostering ADD Talents

Reading about the assets of other ADD adults may help you better understand your own talents—as well as those of your co-workers and loved ones. In recent years, greater numbers of adults who have achieved success in a wide array of fields have been diagnosed with

Yes, ADD Adults Can Be Organized!

Some adults structure their lives around organization to such a degree that the outside world simply can't fathom that they actually have ADD. Contrary to conventional wisdom, the ability to organize is an *asset*—not a deficit—for many ADD adults.

Hannah, a professional organizer in New Jersey, says that people always ask her, "What do you mean you have ADD?" Beginning in childhood, Hannah loved to organize, which she says was a means of compensating for her natural tendencies toward disorganization. "I would always keep a used tissue in my right pocket and a clean tissue in my left," she recalls. "My house was very organized when I was growing up, and I learned from my parents. I love being organized, but I tell people I'm organized because I'm lazy. If I can do things in one step, I won't ever do two steps."

Aaron, a lighting designer, color-coded the filing system for his whole office, which he puns "helped put things in a clearer light!" He says his work helped his co-workers focus better. He thrives on this kind of clarity, and his need for organization made his entire workplace more orderly. In fact, adults with ADD can be the perfect organizers because they implicitly understand what it's like to be disorganized, and they have found ways to overcome this tendency.

ADD. It's clear that the wider world needs to take a more balanced approach to looking at what adults with this condition can offer and which kinds of jobs best suit them and use their special talents.

As the stories of more successful ADD adults reach the mainstream, the effect will most likely be positive. It will no longer be necessary for parents whose children have been diagnosed with the condition to fear that their children won't be productive adults in the work world, and parents can, therefore, take a more studied, informed approach to fostering their children's talents. In addition, adults who are diagnosed with ADD can have a better sense of which type of environment might be a better fit for their unique blend of skills and interests, and they can present their assets to prospective employers with greater clarity and self-confidence.

• ◉ • CHAPTER HIGHLIGHTS • ◉ •

- Adults with ADD may not be able to recognize their strengths, even if they have very real abilities and skills to offer. They may need the help of a friend, career counselor, therapist, or colleague to identify what they do well and to discover how to capitalize on their talents.

- Exercising your talents depends not only on your innate abilities, but also on your environment. You may need to find the right place for your qualities to be appreciated and for you to shine.

- Energy and a willingness to take risks characterize many ADD adults. Their intense energy may lead them to pioneer a new cause or movement and to develop a great number of diverse interests.

- Adults with ADD tend to have empathy for those who learn differently or who are considered different than the norm. This empathy stems partly from their own experience of feeling like they didn't fit into the proverbial mold.

- Many adults with ADD are fearlessly themselves, and they bring a great deal of fun to the workplace. Their sense of fun attracts co-workers and colleagues who find it all too rare in the work world.

- ADD adults think in divergent, creative ways. Their intuitive leaps often result in new creations that previously didn't seem possible.

- The ADD brain can be capable of intense periods of concentration—or "hyperfocusing"—and of paying attention to multiple streams of input at the same time.

- Adults with ADD often have to work harder than everyone else, and they are remarkably determined and diligent as a result.

- Some adults with ADD center their lives around organization to counter their natural tendencies toward disorganization, and they can offer their organizational skills to others. They understand what it means to naturally run to entropy, and they know how to counter this inclination.

PART 2

Finding the Right Career Path

6

Successful ADD Workplaces

> *"It's beneficial to be messy if I'm being creative. James Joyce was messy! Joyce had to have a certain number of cigarette butts in his ashtray."*
>
> —CHARLIE, PHYSICIAN

▉ Follow Your Passion

How can ADD adults find a workplace that suits them? The answer is different for everyone, but it lies partly in following your particular passion. Passion energizes everyone, but it is especially important in keeping ADD adults committed and focused on their work. Their interest in their jobs propels them through periods of lesser activity and excitement and keeps them motivated and concentrated. The ADD brain often needs a greater jolt of interest to keep going, and this can be provided by choosing jobs about which one is excited and by trying to add as much energy and variety to the mix as possible on a daily level.

Vanessa, a public-school teacher with ADD, says it's "doubly important for ADD people to do what they love. Being bored is sudden death. Teaching works for me because it's constant stimulation—it can even be too much. There are twenty people [in my classroom] with different needs and interests, and twenty people to interest me." Vanessa also keeps herself going by teaching many subjects, which involves a great deal of variety. "There's also a lot of challenge because I see the need for constant improvement in what I do."

Sara, a Texas singer/songwriter, has been committed to writing a novel that calls on themes very dear to her heart. "My mom is thrilled and amazed that I've been working on the novel for three years," she says. "I do it consistently every single day. Every morning, I have a ritual. The reason is because this is my life purpose. When you're working for your life purpose, it's a huge driving force."

Scott Eyre, a professional baseball player who pitches for the San Francisco Giants, has loved playing the game since he was a kid, and his passion for baseball has kept him going through the highs and lows in his career. "There are guys who play [professional baseball] who don't watch baseball games on TV," he says. "But I could watch another game right after I play."

But even when you have a job you're passionate about, you're often faced with boring responsibilities such as paperwork. Successful ADD adults have found ways to add spice to mundane tasks by using their outsized powers of creativity. Tom, the director of development at a graduate school, has livened up his writing to make it more interesting, and this helps keep him going. "My reports on donors read like Dickens," he says. "I have to make them interesting, so I write outrageous things about people and go to their core and make the report mine."

Instead of viewing his job as continually asking for money—which could be very wearying—Tom's approach is to listen to people's stories from birth and to find ways to make their dreams come true. "That's the best part of my job," he says. "I love understanding the donors and enjoy letting their stories be told." Using this compelling though unorthodox method, he has closed several multimillion-dollar gifts.

▦ Know What You're Good At

Winona, an actress and filmmaker in Manhattan, consulted with a psychologist who was experienced in working with ADD adults to determine what she's good at. "My therapist kept saying that people with ADD can imagine themselves anywhere, and it's true," Winona says. "For example, I have training in office work, but it's bad for me. People like me—it's never an issue of that—but I couldn't maintain the level of precision and organization needed for office work. I have difficulty looking at a form and copying the information down. It's outrageously difficult for me."

Winona started taking film classes and realized that she was a natural at on-the-spot reporting. "In the first few weeks of film school, I was standing on top of a van filming a marathon. I have no sense that that's dangerous. Jobs that involve physical challenge are great for me. I'm better with a camera running around the city than I am figuring out the structure of a story. I stood out as a cameraperson. I can't follow a script for cues—it's a struggle. But doing things by the seat of my pants is good—anything that needs improvisation. Quick thinking and changes are easier to handle than a set, timed, structured piece."

Winona has an open, artistic mind that gives her the ability to try anything, but she realized that she needed help to figure out the career niche in which she would shine. Even within the same industry—filmmaking—Winona is better at improvisational, adventurous work such as shooting stories than at following set scripts. It took Winona a long time to sort out where she belonged, and she found working with a therapist who's knowledgeable about ADD adults very helpful. Through this structured process, Winona gained insight into her skills and the best places in which to put them to work.

Aaron, a New York lighting designer, has been working with a career counselor who himself has ADD and whom he found on an ADD support group website. Based on what he discovered about himself during the career counseling process, Aaron is considering changing his career. He found working as a lighting designer difficult because the architects on his projects would constantly over-write existing deadlines and make changes that would cause Aaron to be forced to rewrite his specifications for lighting equipment. "I like doing things once," he explains, "and I hate rehashing the same thing. I found it boring. I put a lot of thought and time into things, and it was wasted time."

In reviewing his work history, Aaron realized that he had enjoyed working for a specification catalog for lighting fixtures because "I knew exactly what I had to do on that job." He has used the classic career-search book *What Color Is Your Parachute?* by Richard Nelson Bolles and has created a spreadsheet about how to make and priori-tize career decisions based on his interests and other variables. "I find this very useful because I have a hard time making decisions," he says.

Like Winona, Aaron used a structured career-choice process to determine the vocational path he wanted to follow. Also like Winona, he found a way to use his training—in his case, in lighting design—in a job that was more comfortable and amenable to the way he prefers to work. He is working on finding a new job with-out necessarily going back to school.

Wilma Fellman, who has worked as a career and life-planning counselor for more than twenty years, suggests that adults with ADD who are looking for a new job or career start the process with an extensive data collection process. "Start the process by focusing and collecting your strength areas first and then adding into that mix the areas of challenge," she advises. "Too many career counselors begin backwards—with the disability. In starting with the negative, you're missing the strength and passion that can override some of the challenges."

In her work with ADD adults, Fellman concentrates on finding "all the things that light them up and that are a hand-in-glove fit. That's when the individual starts to say, 'but in me, my ADD is going to mess up the need for sitting for long periods of time and focusing.' Then, we take those negatives and challenges and see if we can match some modifications or strategies to offset that challenge as a negative. We can get really creative," she says, "and most often, if they've got the passion, we can find a way to offset the negative." For more information about working with career counselors, see Chapter 10.

■ Variety and Stimulation

ADD adults may need more stimulation than non-ADD adults to keep them going. One way they provide stimulation is by adding variety to their work lives. ADD coach Becca Gross helps her clients to see that their need for change and for high levels of stimulation, risk, and intensity are positive things. She works with her clients to discover how they can apply these needs to their work. "It may mean a change in lifestyle or job," she says, "or a change in how you see yourself."

Even sedentary jobs can offer the kinds of stimulation ADD adults thrive on if the work is structured in the right way. Margaret, a professor at a liberal arts college, might seem to work in an area that demands too much concentrated study to be attractive to ADD adults, but a closer look at her job reveals why it works for her. "Some aspects of being a college professor are very conducive to ADD," she says. "There's so much multi-tasking, and I can flit from project to project when my attention starts to wander. I have several balls in the air at the same time."

Like Margaret, Rachel, a psychiatrist, always does at least two things at once. Even when she held a full-time job at a prestigious research institution, Rachel also moonlighted sixteen hours a week in a hospital emergency room. Her current job involves many different tasks, including attending on a psychiatry unit, supervising residents, teaching medical students, and carrying out research. This great variety and commitment could positively fatigue a non-ADD adult, but Rachel didn't even realize that she was working a great number of hours until I asked her to estimate how many hours she worked per week.

Will, who works as a producer and A&R person in the New York City R&B and rap music world, finds that he never gets bored. "When you're working on a record, every day brings a new challenge," he says. "There's always something new going on, and it keeps me motivated." These kinds of obstacles might frustrate someone else, but Will says, "what others consider stress, I consider funny." Since he started working at age thirteen, Will "knew there was no way I was going to work 9-to-5."

While many ADD adults thrive on variety and stimulation, they also benefit from working in more organized environments in which they can find the tools they need to leverage their skills and creativity. For example, Brian, now an independent IT consultant, has held many jobs but says the best place he's ever worked in was a very organized financial-services firm. "They had the most resources," he explains. "When you're working on a project, if you have to wait, it's a problem. If you have dedicated resources, it's easier. They also had a well-defined methodology; all the steps of the project life cycle were fully defined and accessible, and they had tons of tools. It was very organized, and it helped a lot," he says.

If you are trying to find the job that provides the right fit for you, it's best to speak with a career counselor who's had experience working with ADD adults. A career counselor who's only worked with the general population may not necessarily understand the particular challenges and needs of people with ADD. For example, an unschooled counselor may not think it's optimal for Winona, the actress described above, to work at two sales jobs while she pursues film studies, but Winona loves variety and movement. The best job she ever had was performing plays in French and English for high schools all around the country as part of a traveling troupe. Because there was a small cast of only eight people, they did everything. Winona took care of the costumes and performed in the play. "I loved it," she recalls. "Doing the same thing in different places was really good. I found something new every day, and I loved traveling. There was consistency but different faces." This need for change and underlying restlessness may require ADD adults to structure their jobs in special ways and to look for work that allows them this kind of movement. It's vital that the career counselor you work with understand these kinds of nuances.

In addition, career counselors who don't work with ADD adults may not understand that serendipity often plays a large role in their career paths and that they tend to have a more circuitous route than the norm. For example, Phil, now a screenwriter, was attending a doctoral program when he found his current path through what he calls "a lark." He was bored at school and invited a Hollywood film actor he admired to speak on campus. The actor had starred in a movie that Phil found "electrifying and magical." Phil felt that the "contrast between how moved he felt by the movie and the flatness of graduate school" was striking, and this got him thinking that he needed to change his career trajectory. Phil spent the weekend hanging out with this actor, and it formed the beginning of a friendship.

Phil developed the idea of remaking an old Preston Sturges film starring his actor friend, but he didn't pursue the project that seriously.

"The line between reasonable and absurd fantasizing is hard to draw," he says. "It's embarrassing to describe [my career path] as so happenstance, but sometimes you stumble on things that call on your aspirations. I wanted to be a writer when I was a child, but my father squashed it out of me. I long since abandoned the idea and pursued goals that weren't going to make me happy."

While searching on the Web, Phil found a hot literary property that he thought could be adapted into an excellent feature film, and he finally gave himself permission to follow his childhood dreams. He's now working on a screenplay that has interest from Hollywood stars.

■ Acceptance from Co-Workers

In Chapter 4, we looked at how adults with ADD can work most productively with their colleagues. Successful ADD employees often rely on co-workers to help them with tasks at which they're not as proficient or that they don't like to do. Acceptance is a crucial element in the workplaces of successful adults, but it's often difficult to find. In the words of Tom, a director of development at a graduate school, "We don't value difference in work environments. It's the same issue as in schooling."

If they can find it, acceptance and openness from co-workers can be a great boon to adults with ADD. For example, Caroline, a computer instructor, finds her current position at a university significantly less stressful than her previous work at a law firm. She feels that she's accepted at her current job, and she has a more intimate relationship with her boss, whom she has told she has ADD. "There's no conflict, so it's a good place for me," she says. "The administration knows I have ADD, so they schedule classes, and I just

Chasing Rewards and "The Proverbial Carrot"

In addition to suceeding by following their passions and dreams, ADD adults do well at jobs that involve continual goodies. ADD coach Jennifer Koretsky suggests that her clients work on commission or at jobs with bonuses and rewards. "The proverbial carrot keeps ADD adults going—knowing that your efforts will pay off," she says.

Eve, an architect and fashion designer, has found it energizing to do something with relatively quick results. When she worked to help design buildings, she found the lengthy lag time between the design and the completion of the project deflating. In comparison with designing buildings, she enjoyed the more immediate results involved in creating a dress for her sister's wedding. "I liked it because I had it in one week," she says. "It felt good when people praised it." She's now considering becoming a full-time fashion designer.

Sara, a singer/songwriter and artist, felt motivated while she was producing a CD because there were many rewards along the way to the finished product. "It's very exciting," she says, "because you want to see it as a finished package. It's never been difficult for me to put recording a CD into movement and to complete it because you get to see it soon, and you see each song completed." Sara found it rewarding to concentrate on milestones along the way to finishing her CD, such as recording single tracks. Building milestones into their work and rewarding themselves for reaching them have helped successful ADD adults stay motivated on their way toward completing larger projects and accomplishing long-term goals.

show up and teach." She also feels more in control because she's not responsible for taking care of details, as she was at the law firm.

Winona, an actress and filmmaker, enjoys working at an herbal store in the East Village, a bohemian section of Manhattan, while she perfects her films. She advises people with ADD to work in this kind of alternative, more open kind of environment. She can arrive five to ten minutes late to work, and she has told her boss that she has ADD. "I've chosen work environments with leeway," she explains. "When I worked as an administrator at a medical office, I couldn't fulfill the responsibilities of the job. I was good with people, but it was incredibly stressful for me. There were too many forms and too much to do."

Feeling accepted allows ADD adults to thrive. In punishing environments, they feel defensive, and their already strong tendency for self-criticism becomes even more virulent when others are offering constant negative feedback. While acceptance is important for all workers, it is especially critical for ADD employees, who may find intolerant workplaces particularly toxic.

■ Productive Workspaces

ADD adults are often very distracted by their work environments. If they work in loud, open spaces, they may not get much done. However, they may also get off track if they are placed in a quiet room on their own. Their physical space requires a great deal of consideration, and they may even want or need to consult with a professional organizer to optimize their workspaces. For more information about how professional organizers work with ADD adults to structure their physical space, see Chapter 10.

In my interviews with successful adults with ADD, I have found that many of them had designed seemingly odd workspaces that provided them with the stimulation they needed to get their work done. For example, Charlie, a physician who writes for pharmaceutical companies from home, works in what he calls a "messy environment. I've cajoled myself with the idea that it's beneficial," he explains. "It's beneficial to be messy if I'm being creative. James Joyce was messy! Joyce had to have a certain number of cigarette butts in his ashtray. It's anxiety-provoking if I'm too neat." Like Charlie, many ADD adults find that the best physical environment for them may be different from what conventional wisdom dictates. They have to find the right amount of stimulation—an optimal balance that gets their creative juices flowing but that doesn't overwhelm them or prevent them or their co-workers from finding what they need.

Sometimes, creating a perfectly silent, neat space may not be the most beneficial way to be productive. ADD coach Jennifer Koretsky gives the example of some ADD adults who don't allow themselves to listen to music while they work—even though it could actually help them. "They don't realize they're not being leisurely but instead doing what they need to do to get their minds going," she says. Listening to music in fact *allows* many ADD workers to concentrate by directing their minds. Instead of scattering their attention among many stimuli, they focus it only on the music and on their work.

Stacey, a teacher and camp consultant, finds that she has to watch television when she gets home to relax. When she was a little girl, her parents took away her television privileges to get her to concentrate on her schoolwork, but it worsened the situation because television is her "salvation. I'm very intense about life," she says. "When I'm home, I 'veg.' TV is my life. For years, I put myself down because I'm addicted to TV, but now I've bought a big-screen TV and accept that this is who I am." While I'm speaking to her on the phone, she has the sound off on her TV but is looking at the pictures.

Many adults mentioned that e-mail, the Internet, or computer games can grab their attention and simply not let go. For example, Margaret, a professor at a liberal arts college in the Midwest, has found that e-mail is the "worst distraction." She used to unplug her computer at work from the Internet, but now that she has wireless Internet, she's always connected. ADD medication helps her concentrate, but e-mail still poses a distraction to her.

Many workers have had to manage these distractions by removing the Internet capabilities from their desktops. Says Phil, a screenwriter, "The Web was invented to destroy lives of people with ADD. It's the ultimate ADD self-medication; you can follow your thoughts wherever they go, and it's organized like the ADD mind. It's a huge distraction. On the other hand, it's not completely unproductive. I'm well informed because I read news on the Web."

Some ADD adults have also designed their jobs to allow them to move around and to be unconstrained by their physical space. Jeff, a computer salesman, has a great deal of physical flexibility on a day-to-day basis. He created a home office in his basement, where he works several days a week. "I can work anywhere with my laptop, cell phone, and DSL," he says. "I'm not chained to my office or to working specific hours as long as my work gets done. My company is very mobile. People dial in on a conference bridge for customer calls, so I don't have to be in my cubicle."

ADD coach Linda Anderson works with her clients to minimize distractions and to take a look at their physical office space. The changes they come up with may be a matter of "the water cooler in the wrong place, or having space to move around in or too much traffic going by." She assists her clients with "making the environment work. But it's not just desk and light, but also a team around you so you can be effective," she says.

•●•CHAPTER HIGHLIGHTS•●•

- Passion energizes everyone, but it is particularly important in keeping ADD adults committed and focused on their work.

- Successful ADD adults often find ways to add spice to mundane tasks by using their outsized powers of creativity.

- Some ADD adults have gained insight into their skills and the best places to make them shine through a structured career-counseling process. For more information about career counseling, see Chapter 10.

- Workers with attention problems may need more stimulation than non-ADD adults to keep them going. One way they provide stimulation is by adding variety to their work lives.

- The "proverbial carrot," including such rewards as bonuses, commissions, and quick results, may help ADD adults stay motivated.

- ADD adults tend to work best in environments in which they feel accepted and in which the levels of unwanted stress aren't high.

- Many ADD adults find that the best physical environment for them may be different from what conventional wisdom dictates. They have to find the right amount of stimulation—an optimal balance that gets their creative juices flowing but that doesn't overwhelm them or prevent them or their co-workers from finding what they need. They may also need to build physical movement and stimulation from music and TV into their work environments.

7

The ADD Leader

"The best boss is able to recognize differences among people and bring the best out of each. We don't value differences in work environments, though. That's why someone with ADD should always be at the head of an organization."
—TOM, GRADUATE SCHOOL DIRECTOR OF DEVELOPMENT

Appreciating Different Viewpoints

A lot of ADD adults wind up working as leaders and thrive in leadership positions because of their open, accepting natures. In Chapter 5, we looked at ways to maximize the strengths that arise from ADD and I discussed how the ADD brain tends to be open to receiving multiple streams of input at the same time. We saw, for example, that Sara, a Texas singer/songwriter who has directed live shows, can listen to the spotlight operator in one ear while speaking to the stage manager in the other. It's not hard, then, to understand how ADD adults in positions of leadership can appreciate input from many people.

Their ability to receive many input streams allows ADD adults to take in one person's ideas without turning away input from others. They can be open to many different truths and ways of being, and this tends to make them more receptive and flexible than most leaders. They are often aware that they can't bring everything to the table, and they're open to the contributions of others who have skills that compensate for some of what they lack. They're usually thankful for the opportunity to work with others who can help keep them on track and ensure that their great ideas are implemented. As a result, groups led by ADD adults may allow others to have more ownership of the results and to enjoy greater professional growth.

For example, Vanessa, a New York City public-school teacher, leads her classroom in ways that empower her students. She admits that she isn't good at the "interior decorator" elements of classroom management. She read that a solution to this problem is to get students involved in helping the teacher manage the upkeep of the classroom. Because she found that she couldn't remember where the classroom materials were stored, Vanessa removed all the doors from the cabinets, and the room, therefore, became more accessible to the students. "The children feel like the classroom is theirs," she says. Vanessa's principal liked this setup so much that she told the custodian to remove the cabinet doors in all the other classrooms in the school.

Scott Eyre, the San Francisco Giants relief pitcher, leads his team on the mound, and he has good, accepting relationships with the whole team. "I'm open," he says. "There are twenty-five guys on the team from other parts of the country and the world, and I'm not biased. I don't treat anyone differently."

■ Collaborative Leadership

The adults whom I interviewed for this book generally enjoyed the exchanges that come from a more democratic style of leadership.

For example, Nick, who is head of staff development at a children's agency in New York City, describes himself as "a very good team player—it's how I do my best work. I see the same qualities in my daughter," he says. "She'll stand up in a soccer field and see the best place to go with the ball. She scans the whole field, and I can do that, too, because I'm caring about fellow persons and compassionate." The director of Nick's agency often threatens workers in a failed attempt to make them more diligent. "It doesn't work," Nick says. "The boss doesn't understand human dynamics. It's better to be reflective and have a back-and-forth with employees."

Nick finds that a lot of his best thoughts come from collaborating with colleagues. He is a part of a discussion group in which members discuss articles about working with young children. "It's about the power of reflective conversation," he says. "Everyone throws ideas in, and the chairperson summarizes what we've learned at the end of our meeting."

Like Nick, Zoe, the sales executive, loves being part of a team, and she particularly enjoys playing a leadership role. "I can accomplish more being on a team," she explains. "There is no situation that doesn't benefit from teamwork. I can learn from everybody, be inspired, and be spurred to think of other things."

ADD adults especially like leading teams that balance their weaknesses and that allow for their full personalities. Says Rachel, a psychiatrist, "I like working on a team when I'm on the top of the team and have a good number-two who's not like me and who I can trust to remind me of what's going on and who can appreciate my positives and negatives." She says that it's important to her that her co-workers understand the particular struggles that stem from working with ADD. "People who haven't worked with a lot of adults with ADD don't get it and don't understand your pain and humiliation when, for example, you've missed an appointment," she explains. "Instead, they come up with suggestions that aren't helpful, or they don't know what to suggest."

The desire of many ADD adults to lead teams arises partly from the sense of control it gives them over their work. Brian, an IT consultant, managed people in one of his previous jobs and says that, "I had a sense of control, and I really liked it. I got to experiment with team-building, and I like that, too."

Leading a team also satisfies ADD adults' willingness to benefit from what others can offer them. Tom, the director of development at a graduate school, says, "the best boss is able to recognize differences among people and bring the best out of each. We don't value differences in work environments, though. That's why someone with ADD should always be at the head of an organization."

It's an interesting idea. In many situations, the best leader is someone who truly accepts that he or she cannot offer everything and is, therefore, more willing to draw on the strengths and contributions of others. This isn't the conventional line of thinking and is another area in which the insights of ADD adults can benefit the wider work world.

▣ Innovation and Energy

In Chapter 5, we saw how the ADD brain can arrive at new insights and make imaginative leaps that leave the rest of the world in the dust. ADD adults bring this same energy and imagination to leadership. In the next chapter, we will look at how ADD adults often find that entrepreneurial ventures provide the perfect outlet for their outsized creative powers.

They also find outlets for their creativity in the right organizations. While working as a physician, Charlie always tried to "do something more creative and express myself." He found that he could be highly self-expressive in his pediatric practice, which he found incredibly rewarding. He joined a new community health organization early in his profession, "and it was delightful to feel like a member of a pioneering group."

Katherine, a disabilities lawyer, wrote a grant to form and fund a center for the practice of disabilities law. Based on her own history, during which she dropped out of high school with undiagnosed ADD and dyslexia and later became a hairdresser, she knew that low-income kids with learning disabilities don't often find their way to higher education, and she pioneered a program to help kids from backgrounds like hers. Even though she found law school extremely difficult and doesn't find the paperwork involved in administrative hearings painless or natural, she was at the top of her class with regard to her great powers of innovation. Very few law school graduates write grants that develop into full-time positions, and very few have the creativity and ability to experiment that allowed Katherine to compensate for her problems in law school by getting books on tape and doing outlines in PowerPoint. ADD leaders like Katherine are often more open and creative, and the result is great innovations that benefit their organizations.

■ Directing Subordinates

ADD adults tend to be forgiving managers because they've previously been on the receiving end of criticism and managerial cruelty. For example, April, a sales consultant, says she has worked with so many tyrants that she knows how horrible it is and doesn't try to replicate the command-and-control style of leadership that has been inflicted on her. Instead, she likes to empower her employees to learn and advance themselves.

Adults with ADD often enjoy team-building but don't generally like disciplining their workers. Howard, a lawyer, has had to manage associates, legal assistants, and secretaries at his firm, but "I hate it," he says. "I don't like being a disciplinarian. First of all, I'm so conditioned to please people, but if you seem wimpy, others will never prioritize what you need. And if you have ADD, it's hypocritical to impose requirements on them that you can't handle. Also, my controls on impulsiveness are not that good, and I have the tendency to say the wrong thing." Howard says that he has over the years developed a "discomfort with hierarchy—I have an egalitarian view of the world."

Caroline, who works as a computer instructor in the New Orleans area, likes managing the flow of her classroom, but she doesn't like directing others in her organization. "I'm afraid they won't do what I tell them. It's hard for me to discipline people, and I have to be more cheerful and optimistic than I am—it's too exhausting."

Not all ADD adults have a difficult time offering constructive criticism. Some tend, in fact, to be outspoken and direct in their feedback to co-workers. Says Rachel, a psychiatrist, "I notice when people do things well, but I'm able to be direct with people about things that aren't going well because it bothers me internally if things aren't right." When Rachel offers critiques of her colleagues' work, she does it in a way that is well-rounded and that recognizes what they're doing well.

Although Rachel considers herself able to bring out the best in others, she often doesn't have time to work on managing them. While she is speaking with me, she mentions that she is sheepishly looking at medical students on the other side of the hospital room. "I want to teach the medical students, but I haven't even gotten my work done yet," she admits. "The things I do well are being empathic, teaching, entertaining, and inspiring people. I bring the best out of people and notice things that people do well. But I'm not good at structuring things, and it's hard to be consistent." Rachel explains that her lack of consistency and structure gets in the way of her finding time to manage people, even if she has the desire and inclination to do so.

Managing others can be too distracting for ADD adults and draws them from their work in unwelcome ways. For example, Caitlin, a litigation attorney, says that she doesn't like to be bothered if subordinates follow up with her. "If what they're bringing me is not on my plate at that moment, I don't want to deal with it," she says. Because she tends to "hyperfocus" on one case—which means directing all her attention only to the task at hand—she is annoyed by assistants who ask her to make decisions on unrelated matters. She says that for that reason, she often can't make the best use of others' help.

Because the brains of ADD adults may not work in the same way as those of their subordinates, ADD leaders sometimes find that others can't follow their leaps in thought. Katherine, a disabilities lawyer in California, finds it difficult to work with more junior attorneys because her thoughts tend to move so quickly. "I really have to be clear in my own head and slow down and explain things to them," she says. She has managed her tendency to make verbal leaps of thought and assume that others understand her. Now, she explicitly tells her employees to let her know if they don't understand her, but, "it's difficult because I'm their boss," she admits. She gives her subordinates permission to interrupt her whenever they need to clarify what she is saying because she understands that her mind may jump ahead of her words.

▦ Setting Expectations for Co-Workers

Some ADD adults have so much energy that they don't understand when their employees or subordinates can't keep up with them. Stacey, who runs her own camp-consulting business, used to employ secretaries before she found that they were too plodding and couldn't match her pace. "My secretary would be on the phone but wasn't doing anything else, and I would go crazy that she wasn't also filing. It's hard for me to work with other people because they can't keep up with me," she says. Stacey now works on her own.

Many ADD adults find that their energy leaves others in the dust. Indeed, while speaking with several of the ADD adults described in this book, I often felt elated but exhausted by their amazing drive and enthusiasm. It was clear to me that they had more energy than the average adult and that they could easily out-power most of their co-workers. It may help to realize that you have higher energy than your co-workers and to set more reasonable expectations for the way others choose to work. For example, the average worker may not be able to multitask or to work as long as you can on projects that interest you.

■ Perfectionism: A Double-Edged Sword

ADD adults often direct their overwhelming energy toward making their work perfect, but this kind of perfectionism may slow down their work and irritate their colleagues. As a result, leaders with ADD often use their great innovative powers to initiate projects, but the completion of their work is problematic. This is often confusing and debilitating for those who follow ADD leaders. Subordinates tend to flock to ADD leaders to push through the brainstorming and other exciting parts of a project, only to find that the work gets bogged down when the leader continually frets over the project in a futile attempt to perfect it.

Charlie, a physician with ADD, has taken the lead writing role on marketing projects for pharmaceutical companies. Recently, he worked on a series of websites that were designed to train sales representatives on how a specific drug is used. He produced an out-line that was approved by his clients, and he was supposed to fill out this outline to quickly produce the finished product. Instead, he be-gan re-doing the outline from scratch. His contacts at the pharma-ceutical company began to complain, and Charlie had to curb his impulses to rip up the original draft. He recognized the error of his ways, but he still often feels tempted to continually start anew. "I see an outline only as an exploration of ideas," he explains.

ADD leaders are often inclined to keep working on an idea until it's perfect, rather than to push toward the completion of the project and by definition stint a bit on the quality of their work in response to time pressures. Jennifer Koretsky, an ADD coach, has noted that many of her clients, including leaders and entrepreneurs, have trou-ble with a particular breed of perfectionism. Even though others think they're done, ADD adults still find something else to change. "It's more of a shifting problem," she says, explaining that once they've completed one stage of a process, some ADD adults are unable to then shift their attention to something else. "You have to say 'I've done the best I can do' and shift your attention elsewhere," she says.

Charlie, the physician, found that the most helpful boss he ever had kept him from stalling on work by continually telling him what was needed and whether Charlie was providing it. "I came to under-stand my shortcomings," Charlie says. "It was painful but helpful." Therefore, ADD employees like Charlie can benefit from others who keep them accountable and who keep them moving, even if they feel like going back to perfect an earlier part of the process.

■ Future Exploration About ADD Leaders

Not much has been written about ADD leaders because most haven't realized or told others that they have this condition. As more

adults are diagnosed and feel comfortable coming out of the proverbial ADD closet, we will have a better understanding of the
strengths they offer and the challenges involved in working with and
for them.

Working for an ADD Boss

If you work with an ADD boss (or a boss whom you strongly suspect has ADD),
the information in this chapter may help you better understand how to appreciate what your supervisor can offer and the ways in which you may have to
back up the person. You should realize that adults with ADD tend to be open
to new ideas and to working with several streams of input at once. Just because they accept your co-worker's idea, that doesn't mean that they also
won't accept yours; if they accept your idea, don't be surprised if they still
ask for more input from others.

You may also want to work out a system with your supervisor whereby you
ask him or her if it's all right to periodically clarify directions and you offer
to schedule and remind him or her of tasks. Generally, ADD leaders don't
mind getting this kind of help as long as you understand who they are and
how they operate and are open yourself to new ways of thinking and being. If
you offer help in a thoughtful, compassionate way, the evidence from the
people interviewed for this book is that your boss is likely to accept it. This,
of course, may be difficult if you feel annoyed by your boss's previous
mishaps and forgetfulness, but the result may be a workplace that runs more
smoothly for everyone and that is a generally more pleasant and productive
place in which to work. The study of ADD leadership is ongoing because not
many adults identify themselves as having ADD in the workplace due to the
perceived stigma attached to it. As more ADD leaders emerge, we will have
a clearer picture of the most productive ways to work with them.

Many of the adults interviewed for this book said that their sub-ordinates probably suspected that "they ain't right," in the words of one. However, because many individuals have been reluctant to tell co-workers they have ADD, we can't yet examine in any meaning-ful way their leadership patterns from the point of view of their subordinates.

• ● • CHAPTER HIGHLIGHTS • ● •

- ADD leaders tend to be receptive to multiple sources of infor-mation. They enjoy working with others who can compensate for their weaknesses and who appreciate their strengths.

- ADD adults often pioneer new movements and spearhead inno-vations using their great creative powers.

- Leaders with ADD sometimes find it difficult to discipline sub-ordinates because they have been on the receiving end of a great deal of criticism in the past. When they give criticism, they tend to offer well-rounded, direct feedback.

- Some ADD supervisors find it difficult to manage others be-cause it involves working out schedules and plans in advance. They also find that they tend to make intuitive leaps that may be inexplicable to their subordinates. It's often helpful for ADD bosses to give their co-workers permission to ask if they don't understand their directions.

- Many ADD adults are very high energy and may not understand why their assistants and co-workers can't keep up with them. Keeping in mind your subordinates' limitations, as well as their strengths, is useful and may help you balance your own deficits and talents. In managing others, it may help to realize that your energy level is often unusual in its power and duration.

- Leaders with ADD may also benefit from working with people who can counteract their tendency to want to work persistently and to perfection on one part of a project—even if there isn't time for it.

- Most ADD leaders don't explicitly tell those who work with them that they have ADD. Therefore, there isn't a great deal of information on how to work best with an ADD boss. This is an area for further study.

- If you work for an ADD boss, you may be annoyed at his or her mishaps, but there is ample reason to believe that your boss will welcome thoughtful suggestions about and help in managing time and tasks.

8

The ADD Entrepreneur

"The profile of people who do well in entrepreneurship is similar to the profile of people with ADD—they don't tend to like people telling them what to do."

— BONNIE MINCU, A BUSINESS COACH
WHO SPECIALIZES IN ADD ADULTS

■ ADD and Entrepreneurship: A Good Fit

David Neeleman, the CEO and founder of JetBlue Airways, can't sit still. Now in his forties, he was recently diagnosed with ADD. He flies at least once per week on one of his planes because he gets restless sitting at his desk. The result is an airline that's incredibly responsive to his customers and their energy. He recently found out from customers that they needed more leg room, and he removed the last row of seats, which weren't able to recline. When he found out his customers wanted low-carbohydrate foods, he added almonds to the snacks available on JetBlue planes.

When you fly on JetBlue, you can sense the difference. At the hub at JFK Airport in New York City, the ticket counters have large-screen televisions to amuse you while you wait in line, and each seat—even in coach—comes with twenty-four free channels of

DIRECTV®. It's clear that Neeleman is a man who understands boredom and wants to spare his customers the frustration of tedious flights. In turn, consumers clearly appreciate Neeleman's understanding of their restlessness and their desire for a playful, fun airline. Since its launch in February 2000, JetBlue has grown from two planes to twenty-seven cities and 238 daily flights, with more destinations added each year. Neeleman thinks differently from the average CEO, but it's clear that what he does works.

JetBlue is only Neeleman's latest venture in an entrepreneurial career that began in his twenties. He started Morris Air in Utah and later sold it to Southwest Airlines. He tried working at Southwest but found that it wasn't receptive to his innovations, so he developed Open Skies, the first e-ticketing system, and helped start WestJet, a discount airline in Canada.

As David Neeleman's career shows, entrepreneurship and ADD can fit together quite well. In a recent study, researchers found that 18 percent of adults with ADD owned their own businesses, as compared to 5 percent of the non-ADD group.[1] The authors of this study explain their results by pointing out that children with ADD tend to have difficulty in school and that when they become adults, they either lack sufficient education to reach higher positions, or they try to avoid the need for higher education by going into business for themselves. Another recent study found that fully one third of ADD adults become entrepreneurs by age thirty.

---

[1] Carroll, C. B., & Ponterotto, J. G. (1998). Employment counseling for adults with attention-deficit/hyperactivity disorder: Issues without answers. *Journal of Employment Counseling, 35,* 79–96.

■ A Different Way of Thinking

Bonnie Mincu, a New York City business coach who specializes in ADD adults, says that "ADD adults tend to think like entrepreneurs. The profile of people who do well in entrepreneurship is similar to the profile of people with ADD—they don't tend to like people telling them what to do."

ADD entrepreneurs tend to capitalize on the following qualities, which they have in abundance:

• Creativity

• Great energy

• The inclination to take risks

• The ability to see what doesn't already exist

• The willingness to embrace change

Entrepreneurship is a way in which ADD adults can find creative paths to leverage their immense powers of innovation and the other qualities mentioned above. They often feel bored at conventional jobs, and they need the flexibility and variety afforded by going out on their own to flex their huge creative muscles.

Brian is a great example of someone who had to go out on his own to keep his creative batteries charged. He became an independent IT consultant after years of working at jobs in which he generally got burned out after about a year. "I had at least three times the number of jobs of anyone I know," he says about his work history. He describes consulting as a "good fit" because "there's a cycle each project follows and different activities in each phase; each project has its own problems. When things wind down, I get bored quickly."

He has tailored his work life to fit the natural expansions and contractions of his interest level. "Once the new software has been implemented, the issues you deal with are mundane and the rush to the finish line is over, so I usually roll off the project at that point," he says.

ADD adults also find entrepreneurship attractive because they tend to be egalitarian and not invested in hierarchies. Says Howard, a lawyer who was recently diagnosed with ADD, "there's an assumption we [Americans] have internalized that those who reap disproportionate rewards must have disproportionate talents, such as Jack Welch or Bill Gates, but I'm skeptical of giving these people the distinction of genius." Howard doesn't feel that leaders should take all the credit for efforts that involve a great number of others who toil along with them. He says, "in the past, invention was viewed as a more collective process. It's rare for inventions to be the brainchild of one person—lots of people work on it."

Because he likes to work on his own, Howard left his San Francisco law firm to become a free agent, and he now works on a project-to-project basis. "It has allowed me to only work with people I like," he says, "because they're the ones who give me work."

Although entrepreneurship is a good match with the restless, democratic nature of ADD adults, the lack of structure that goes along with striking out on one's own poses particular problems for them. The most successful entrepreneurs with ADD set up systems that enable them to do what they're best at, while leaving others to manage the details. Linda Anderson, an ADD coach, says that one of the major goals of her work with entrepreneurs is to "get the client to delegate and to know what their pitfalls are." She says that the qualities that make ADD adults great entrepreneurs can also, paradoxically, stymie them. "They tend to spread themselves too thin and can pursue too many ideas at a time," she explains.

In this chapter, we will look at some of the problems faced by

ADD adults who strike out on their own professionally and examine how successful entrepreneurs have handled these challenges.

■ Delegating and Getting Help

ADD coach Jennifer Koretsky tells her entrepreneurial clients, "You don't have to be good at everything." She suggests that if her clients have a trusted partner in business or at home who can take over something they don't like to do or aren't good at, it's acceptable for this other person to take over that part of the work. She advises her clients to delegate tasks such as proofreading and finances that will get in the way of doing what they really want to do.

ADD entrepreneurs tend to struggle with the more routine aspects of their work while thriving on the more challenging parts of their businesses. For example, Sean is a $150,000-a-year independent international business consultant who works out of the Boston area. Despite his success, he finds it difficult to manage all the tasks associated with his consulting practice. "I'm better at getting on an airplane than being an accountant, writing a proposal, or sending out bills," he admits. Sean manages to complete these backup functions himself by using a variety of calendars, focusing on his deadlines, and setting his watch twenty minutes ahead to combat his tendency to be fifteen minutes late. Still, he finds that he often can't concentrate. "My mind is all over the place, and it causes problems." He also misses the collegiality of working in an office and the daily regimen and stimuli it provides. "I work better in a team," he says. "It's hard to be a lone ranger."

Sean's extraordinary talents have enabled him to overcome obstacles that could have interfered with his success. "I used to stutter badly," he tells me in perfectly fluent prose accompanied by a chuckle, "but now I'm paid $3,000 a day as a presenter."

While some entrepreneurs like Sean force themselves to slog through the details, even if they are not to their liking, others gladly outsource these distasteful duties. April, a Texas-based sales consultant, enjoys letting her assistant, lawyer, and accountant handle the tasks she doesn't like or that don't particularly match her aptitudes.

When I ask April if she has structured her company in a way that works well for her, she answers without hesitation, "You bet!" She explains, "I'm very organized. I have files set up, and my assistant manages them. I hate filing, so my assistant does it, and I have other processes in place. I write down what I need for supplies, and my assistant gets them." April is also considering hiring a business coach to consult with about her business processes.

Sometimes, ADD entrepreneurs would like to delegate unwanted tasks but can't impose the structure necessary to organize their work to pass it off to someone else. Says Lois, an artist who has come up with an idea for a line of toys, "It's difficult to delegate if you can't figure out steps A, B, and C." She is thinking of hiring a firm to manufacture her toys, but she has found that it's been nearly impossible to get to the point of figuring out what she needs to do to select the right manufacturer. In the past, a coach helped her prioritize her actions, but she's not using a coach now because she doesn't have the money.

Because she has been unable to get past this roadblock, Lois is tired of working alone and feels that the time is right to hire others to help her get to the next step. "I'm good at conceptualizing things and bringing them to a certain level, but I need a team to help me take my projects into the world," she says. At this point in her business, she would like to get a team together to bring her toys to market. A large children's store chain was interested in her product, but she couldn't capitalize on this opportunity because she still wasn't sure how to go about acquiring the team to get her toys to the shelf.

▪ Handling Stress, Monitoring Your Progress, and Getting Things Done

When you are unhappy at your 9-to-5 job, entrepreneurship may seem like the ideal solution to your cranky boss and dull routine. From afar, working for yourself may appear relatively stress-free. However, most of the entrepreneurs interviewed for this book seemed saturated with anxiety, even years after they'd gone out on their own.

In fact, ADD entrepreneurs may feel more anxious about their progress in such areas as generating new business than they really have to be. Part of this chronic stress is due to their feeling of never measuring up, no matter what they achieve (a common ADD problem that may require therapy for its resolution or alleviation), and this anxiety may also arise from their lack of good controls. That is, due to poor bookkeeping and goal-setting, self-employed ADD adults may not know how much they're bringing in and they may not have established goals to monitor their progress. As a result, they feel like they're floating through space without being able to measure if they've really been successful or not. In the absence of good planning and realistic goals, they may not know which yardsticks to use and, consequently, they feel lost and confused. It's almost as if they are trying to chart their progress across a vast ocean without having identified the landmarks that will signify that they've finally arrived—or at least have reached the midway point.

For example, it took Lois, a self-employed artist, ten years before she stopped feeling anxious about having work coming in because it was only after all this time that she realized she'd been self-employed successfully and could reliably support herself. Only the fact that she'd been getting by for ten years convinced her that she wasn't a failure because she had no other standard by which to measure her progress and she uses an erratic control process. She also tends to feel buffeted about by the feast-or-famine cycles of self-employment that either leave her too idle or far too busy.

Since launching her business, Lois hasn't kept good track of her clients. At one point, she made a card for each client and updated it each time she had contact with the client over the years, but she has stopped doing that. She doesn't consistently monitor her business's progress, and she says she needs to keep better track of her finances.

In addition to setting up controls, ADD adults also need to establish realistic goals and understand what they can get done in a certain amount of time. Their appreciation for how long things will take may be flawed, and this may leave them dissatisfied with what they've done—even if it's actually a great deal. For example, Sara, the self-employed Texas singer and songwriter, has so much energy that she will look at her accomplishments and think she hasn't done anything, while others look at her and think it's absolutely unbelievable what she can get done. "The list of what I want to do is much longer than what I can accomplish," she says. "What I write down for a half a day, others write down for a week." Working with a coach, she began to realize what it was realistic for her to do in a given period of time, and now she feels better about her achievements. "Now that I have more realistic time management, I feel a greater sense of accomplishment," she says.

Collaborating with a coach, friend, or partner may help adults with ADD set and achieve more appropriate goals, and it may also reduce their anxiety about their progress and achievements. If they are using an unreasonable yardstick to measure their progress, they may forever feel inadequate. In addition, accurate and consistent accounting will help them figure out if they're meeting their financial goals. For more information about working with an ADD coach, see Chapter 10.

Using controls and setting goals becomes even more important for entrepreneurs over time. Often, getting the business off the ground isn't the hard part for ADD adults, as they are burning with passion and energy that provide a powerful jump-start to their projects; instead, they need help implementing systems and processes that keep the business running smoothly as time goes on. The trick is dealing with the more mundane details once the exciting initial launch has occurred. ADD coach Linda Anderson describes her clients as "great initiators, but they need help sorting out what's most important and what to prioritize."

Coach Jennifer Koretsky has noticed that her self-employed clients have difficulty establishing financial goals and planning. She suggests that they devote one day per week to going through their financial records and staying on top of them. This builds consistency into their schedules and allows them to be sure they devote time to the necessary detail work that may be overlooked in their quest to do the more exciting tasks that inspired them to work on their own in the first place.

Over time, ADD adults often accept that using controls and monitoring processes are helpful, even if they aren't second nature. For example, April, the sales consultant, worked in sales at another organization for a boss whom she thought was a tyrant. The boss called her every morning to see if she was out of bed, and she eventually quit, tiring of working under what she considered his "Gestapo" style of management. However, when she went to work for another company, she found that her former boss's processes and systems worked really well for her. To this day, she still uses the systems she learned from her former "Gestapolike" boss, and she credits these controls with keeping her business on track. In fact, she is such a convert to the need for controls that she teaches these practices to her clients through her sales consulting practice. Years later, her once-dreaded former boss apologized to her and explained that he'd been going through a personal crisis when April had worked for him. He then hired her as a consultant to implement in his current organization the same work processes that he had taught her when they had worked together in the past.

■ Perfectionism and Getting Stuck

ADD coach Jennifer Koretsky has worked with a lot of entrepreneurs for whom perfectionism is problematic. We saw the ADD tendency to aim for perfection in the previous chapter on ADD leaders, so it's no surprise that the same tendency bedevils those adults who go out on their own. In fact, it might be even more problematic for entrepreneurs because they often don't have coworkers who keep them moving and who override their tendency to get stuck trying to perfect one stage of a long project. It can also be hard for ADD entrepreneurs to delegate because they often want to control everything and be sure it turns out well.

Sometimes, what looks like perfectionism—or the tendency to try to perfect one step before going on to the next—actually results from feeling overwhelmed. Lois, the self-employed artist, fears taking her business plans about starting a children's toy line to the next level because the demands of the next step are so daunting and flood her with anxiety. "I have a lot of ideas, but I'm overwhelmed about what it involves," she explains.

Sara, the Texas singer and songwriter, is often overwhelmed when she starts a project, but a coach she worked with a few years ago gave her tools to get beyond that stage. "I would feel overwhelmed by everything that had to be done and couldn't get started. My brain is so full of so many ideas that I can't grab onto one and make it concrete," she says. "My coach would let me talk and work it out while talking about it. The weeding-out process happens as I'm talking. I realize that some of the ideas ping-ponging around in my head aren't valid. Then I can get out a list and write them down. As I see the list, I can say, 'That would be really nice, but that's not going to happen.' I'll cross it off, and it's totally okay."

Working through the great rush of ideas in their heads with a trusted colleague or coach allows ADD adults to sort out the wheat from the chaff and move beyond the exploratory stage to implementing a select group of the great ideas they've come up with.

■ Structure and Balance

Although the freelance life allows ADD adults to capitalize on moments of increased productivity and to accomplish things their own way, it can also leave them stranded in a world with too few supports and too little structure in which they tend to flounder. ADD coach Becca Gross helps her entrepreneurial clients build structure along with flexibility into their work days, which can at times be a difficult balancing act. Gross asks her clients the times of day during which they work best, and she tries to help them build schedules that leverage their periods of greatest attention.

Independent workers with ADD find that their work often goes better if they impose their own structure on their days or their tasks. Sam, who works as an independent painter and carpenter, tries to structure his time by breaking his work into smaller chunks. "I try to time myself so I work just so many hours and not longer," he says. "Otherwise, I tend to obsess and do too much at once and get burned out. There's usually a logic to how I approach a job. I try to do the first things first, like woodwork—there's an order to it. I have to prime top to bottom, left to right. I'm most successful if I work in a rigid fashion."

Sometimes, solo practitioners need the stimuli of others, and even people who enjoy working at home at times need to be around other people. Caroline, a computer instructor and freelance consultant, likes working at her home in the New Orleans area, but she finds that her house can often be too quiet for her. During these times, she begins worrying about her income. To distract herself, she needs stimulation and heads to her local coffee shop for the noise and temporary relief from worry that it provides.

Rosa, an aspiring Hollywood screenwriter, uses a writers' group to keep her accountable. She has found that this system speeds her along toward finishing her screenplays. Rosa took an extension class at a local university to get a rewrite done. Because she had just relocated to the West Coast, it helped her meet people, and it gave her a structure of dates by which she had to complete her screenplay. "I hand in everything on time," she says. "If I commit, I will do that or feel guilty—it's my Catholic upbringing."

She has also developed a structured writing process by which her first draft concentrates on the vertical outline, or the character development, while the next draft looks at the horizontal layer, or the plot. "If I don't do that, I'm looking at it as an overwhelming beast," she says. "I usually have six ideas I want to work on and can't let go and focus on one."

Sometimes self-employed ADD adults find it difficult to stop working. This tendency creates a workaholic lifestyle in which their careers and business pursuits take over. Linda Anderson, an ADD coach, tries to curb the workaholic natures of some of her entrepreneurial clients. "I help them sort out their priorities and achieve balance in their life if they work all the time," she says. "An entrepreneur with ADD can be all over the place."

Often, curbing their natural tendency to get involved in too many things requires ADD adults to consciously realize that they tend to overcommit and to give themselves permission not to do so. In the last several years, Sara, the Texas singer and songwriter, has "allowed myself not to operate in the way society says we have to operate. We have to be really busy all the time, but I don't put my-self in those situations." Sara is working on writing a novel, record-ing a CD, and teaching adult education classes through church and community groups. Though she's been asked to teach additional classes, she's gotten really good at declining these opportunities. It used to be very difficult for her to draw limits around her time, but now she doesn't impulsively commit every time she's asked to do something. She has a greater sense of how much time she has, and she has decided that her priority is having time to work on her novel.

ADD coach Jennifer Koretsky sees a lot of entrepreneurial clients who are positively besieged with new ideas and can't find peace. "These are really the ideas people," she says. "They have so many ideas coming in. I tell them to take time to recharge every day through meditation or through taking a long walk. It helps them figure out which ideas are worth pursuing and take action on them."

In other words, ADD adults are often blessed with too much of a good thing. Allowing their ideas to blossom necessarily involves limiting how many of their ideas they follow up on and taking time to smell the proverbial flowers to recharge their batteries.

Using Creativity to Market Yourself

Entrepreneurs with ADD benefit from setting aside a day every week or two to call potential clients and drum up new business. This allows them to dedi-cate time to a vital function that keeps their businesses going.

continued . . .

Sara, the singer/songwriter, chooses a day to call potential clients, but it's often hard for her to pick up the phone to make the first call. "I will do everything to distract myself and not get started," she admits.

To conquer her inertia about promoting her business, she infused the marketing campaign for her band with great creativity. Going beyond the mundane and crafting a truly original marketing campaign helped inspire her to get moving. Instead of simply stapling her band poster around the neighborhood, as many bands do, she produced a lively newsletter with pictures of her band recording in the studio. Her dog, a wire hair fox terrier, was featured as the editor in the humorously written newsletter. She still had a hard time making calls to scrounge up ads for the newsletter, but the creativity of her project powered her through it. "I had to buck up for the day I made calls," she admits, "but I would always sell eight ads quarterly that paid for the printing and mailing." Her newsletter helped attract people to her act and made clubs and recording companies more aware of her band.

Sara used her creativity—a common ADD strength—to inspire herself to get moving on a task she found tedious and to drum up business for her band. Going beyond the obvious and calling on their natural innovative powers may help ADD entrepreneurs muster the energy for tasks such as marketing that may at first appear boring. For more information on how to network and market your products and services, see Chapter 4.

• ● • CHAPTER HIGHLIGHTS • ● •

- ADD and entrepreneurship often go hand-in-hand. It is estimated that there is a disproportionate number of self-employed ADD adults in the United States in relation to their percentage of the total adult population.

- ADD entrepreneurs often find it useful to identify their pitfalls or potential weaknesses and to enlist trusted partners to help them with the areas that they aren't as good at or that they don't like.

- Entrepreneurs with ADD sometimes feel anxious about their progress because they have set unrealistic goals and are afraid they can't measure up to them. They are often helped by working with a coach or partner to establish more realistic goals and to set up consistent internal processes that enable them to monitor their progress toward these goals.

- Often, ADD adults with great ideas are stymied in moving on to the next step because they feel overwhelmed or strive for perfect results. If they consult a trusted adviser or friend, they can feel more in control and ready to move on to turning their good ideas into action.

- Entrepreneurship allows for greater flexibility—which is at once a blessing and a burden. It allows adults with ADD to maximize their periods of greatest productivity and to achieve results in their own ways, but it also requires them to establish accountability and structure to keep their days on track.

- ADD entrepreneurs can allow work to take over their lives. They need times of lesser concentration and relaxation to keep their lives balanced and to recharge themselves.

- Entrepreneurs with ADD are also helped by setting aside time for marketing and generating new business. Their great powers of creativity can help them market their services in ways that get them noticed and that inspire them to carry out their campaigns. For more information on marketing and networking, see Chapter 4.

9

What if You're Not the CEO?

> *"My most helpful boss always took me under his wing. He got it that I loved my work, that it was fun for me. He always challenged me, but not in a negative way."*
>
> —APRIL, SALES CONSULTANT

■ Working Well with Your Boss

In the previous chapter, we saw that adult ADD and entrepreneurship are incredibly complementary. But what if you work in a large organization and aren't able to call on your subordinates to help you complete your work and ensure that your great ideas are carried out? This chapter helps you find ways to work productively even if you don't have the ability to hire people to remedy your deficits. There are still ways to find a boss who can provide the structure you need. In addition, this chapter addresses ways to ask your employer for accommodations that will allow you to work better.

Managers: A Double-Edged Sword

Managers are a double-edged sword for ADD adults. Bosses provide a vital function in keeping their workers on track, but adults with ADD often resist being told what to do and desire a great deal of freedom in how they accomplish their work. This chapter examines the traits of a productive manager for ADD adults and looks at how ADD employees can work best with their bosses.

The Worst Managers: Unsympathetic Tyrants

When interviewing successful ADD adults, I always ask them to describe the least helpful managers they've ever worked with. The bosses they love to hate are, in their subordinates' words, "a tyrant," "Gestapo," "a screamer," "unsympathetic," and "closed." These Lucifers of the work world answered their employees' interested questions about why they were pursuing a certain course of action with a terse "because" and called every morning to see if their employees had gotten out of bed. They were hard to please but never explained exactly what they wanted. They either provided too many directions or far too few.

Michelle, a social worker in Tennessee, describes the least helpful boss she's ever had as "extremely demanding, but she gave me no outline of the protocol and left me to my own devices to know how to function. When I didn't do the right thing, she humiliated me and then terminated me. She was very shaming and not approachable. I couldn't tell her I needed help."

When I ask Caroline, a computer instructor, about the worst boss she's ever had, she replies that unfortunately, "There have been several of those." One of her least helpful bosses issued directions to Caroline as she walked by Caroline's desk, but this supervisor didn't want Caroline to write down her tasks. "This boss would never ask me how things were going, or if I needed help," Caroline adds.

Caroline told this boss that she had ADD and asked for accommodations to help her excel at her job. When her manager would not change the office rules, Caroline told her that she was violating the Americans with Disabilities Act (ADA), a federal law that states that workers who are otherwise able to do the job must by law receive necessary accommodations (with some stipulations about their cost). Caroline also wrote a letter to this effect, but her boss grew even angrier in response to the letter, and Caroline wound up leaving her job with five weeks' pay as a result.

Rachel, a psychiatrist, describes her least helpful boss as a person who threw too much her way without explaining it. "This person gave instructions that were too quick. My least helpful bosses have provided either too much structure or too little. It's also not good if the boss says, 'Do A, B, C.'" Rachel desired a bit of wiggle room in how she accomplished her work; even if her methods were at times unconventional, she wanted to be evaluated on the product, not on her own idiosyncratic process.

ADD coach Linda Anderson has helped many clients discover what works for them in their job environment. Though each adult is different and each person's needs vary, Anderson says it's essential that employees with ADD work with a manager who provides them with what she calls a "container." This means that the manager must establish helpful rules and regular meetings to be sure the employee stays on track. "[ADD adults] are lost trying to do it all by themselves," she says. "They need boundaries in the job and someone to give them reflection. A good boss checks in, creating a container and responsibility without micro-management. The boss says, 'Let's talk about what's going on so we know we're on track.'"

Now that we know what doesn't work, let's now look at how ADD adults described their most helpful bosses.

The Ideal Boss: Open Yet Structured

When I ask the same successful adults working with ADD to describe the most helpful boss they've ever had, a clear composite begins to emerge. The ideal manager for these people is democratic yet firm, open yet structured. He or she allows the ADD adult to accomplish the job in his or her own way, yet provides guidance when needed. In short, this type of boss tows a middle path and is flexible enough to allow the person to get his or her work done while providing the structure to be sure the worker keeps on track.

The best bosses recognize the strengths of their ADD employees, accept them for who they are, and work to provide accountability in gentle ways. "The best boss I ever had was able to recognize differences among people and bring the best out of each," says Tom, a graduate school director of development. "He didn't blame people for problems."

April, a sales consultant, describes her best manager as a kind of coach. "My most helpful boss always took me under his wing. He got it that I loved my work, that it was fun for me. He always challenged me, but not in a negative way. I felt comfortable to go to him, and I asked him as a mentor about an opportunity to go off on my own. He guaranteed that I could come back if it didn't work out." Decades later, April is successful as an independent sales consultant and thanks this former boss for his support that enabled her to spread her wings and be successful on her own. Zoe, a sales executive, says that her most helpful boss "was funny and fun and real," which was important to her because "I don't like the corporate environment."

ADD employees do best with managers who are clear in their directions and who provide constant gentle prodding to get work done. Charlie, a physician, says the best boss he ever had "kept telling me what he needed and where I wasn't providing it. I came to understand my short-comings. It was painful but helpful."

Based on the comments of these adults, we get a picture of the best boss not as a touchy-feely, Polyanna type, but as someone who takes a full, nuanced look at the employee and who honestly—but kindly—helps him or her work up to potential. For example, Jeff, a computer salesman, describes the best boss he's ever worked with as "a manager and a coach. He wouldn't hesitate to tell you if you were screwing up, but he'd also tell you what to do to fix it." Jeff learned a lot from this man about how to perfect his customer-service skills, and he credits these skills with enabling him to keep his job and prosper during the high-tech downturn when his company was letting people go left and right.

Managers may also find it more productive if they provide their ADD employees with written instructions. Aaron, the lighting designer, says, "I get about 70 percent of what my bosses say. The other amount is lost, so I prefer things in writing. If my bosses don't write it down, I will."

If Caroline, a computer instructor, is worried that she may not be doing the right thing at work, she makes a bee-line to her supervisor to receive explicit directions "rather than make the wrong guess." She has told her supervisor that she has ADD, and that has helped her. "I've been straightforward," Caroline says. When she's speaking with her boss, "I tell her I have to get out my calendar and write things down."

Helpful managers also recognize that ADD adults may have strange lacunae, or gaps, in their skill sets. For example, Rachel, an accomplished psychiatrist who has carried out complex research studies, has difficulty reading schedules. She made a nearly career-ending mistake when she read a schedule incorrectly and didn't realize that she was on call and left the hospital. After telling her bosses that she had ADD, it actually allayed some of her supervisors' concerns. "They may have been concerned I was impaired or using substances," she says. Before that time, she'd experienced similar forgetful incidents and had always been met with the response from her supervisors of "How could you?" She recalls that even though she was a great student in high school, her teachers reacted with disbelief when she forgot her homework, so it was a relief to tell her supervisors that she had ADD and meet with understanding about how that would affect her.

The ideal boss for ADD workers is also supple in his or her approach and provides flexibility in the context of structure. This type of boss lets employees reach their goals in their own unique ways. For example, Vanessa, a New York City public school teacher, says that she wants "someone who will tell her what to do. I need supervision, but then I want the principal to leave me alone to do it on my own. But I'm not good at reading body cues, so if I don't get direct feedback, I won't know what to do on my own." She said that while she needs direct feedback, she also requires a great deal of positive feedback. "I know I'm smart, so why can't I do things?" she asks.

The conscientious manager of ADD adults may face a difficult path in trying to hew an elusive middle ground between structure and flexibility. Overall, the manager will get the best out of ADD employees if he or she has an insight into what it feels like to be constantly aware of one's shortfalls. The boss's understanding of the ADD adult's often bruised ego that stems from a lifetime of feeling insecure and insufficient will help him or her in guiding the employee forcefully but kindly. This is something that most employees, even those without ADD, are looking for in a boss, but it's particularly critical for the productive management of ADD adults.

▪ Accepting Criticism and Feedback

ADD adults tend to find it helpful if their managers contribute structure and guidance to keep their work on track, but their bosses must do this without making the employee feel singled out or unfairly criticized. ADD adults have a long history of being criticized and scolded by their parents, teachers, and employers for failing to do things on time or the "right way." They may not have strong feelings of self-worth, and the boss's honest feedback, even if well-intentioned, may draw on the ADD employee's deep well of self-doubt and put him or her in a defensive posture. In addition, a common characteristic of people with ADD is to concentrate on the negative, so they may remember balanced feedback in an entirely negative way.

Many adults with ADD find it difficult to receive any type of feedback. Stacey, a physical education teacher for special education students, says she's "not good with confrontation or when someone questions me. If I'm doing my job, leave me alone." She says she doesn't tend to do well working for other people, and she has managed to work part-time at two different schools and arrange her jobs so she comes and goes as she pleases without answering to supervisors.

Vanessa, a public-school teacher, generally reads a book if she has a work-related problem that she wants to resolve because she can't always accept feedback from others. "My first solution is to read a book if I have a problem because it's not interpersonal. I have trouble learning from others because I feel judged. I'm very afraid of negative comments even if I hear lots of positive. If I hear one negative, I concentrate on it. Books don't judge me."

Ben, a computer usability engineer, says his best boss "wasn't authoritarian and allowed me to use my talents and abilities the way I learned them." Ben is very bright but found that in school, he learned differently from other people. As a result, "it's easier to be judged on results rather than on how I follow a process." Ben doesn't tend to thrive in work environments "with a lot of strict deadlines and oversight involved and if someone is always checking, and I have to explain how I do things." He says, "It's much easier to do the work in a more creative matter and be judged on the results."

Managers who rely on textbook methods may find their ADD employees wanting. However, if they concentrate on the results, they may realize that they're getting what they want and that their ADD employees contribute new ways of doing things that work well.

Accentuate the Positive

In evaluating your relationship with your manager, it may be helpful to keep in mind that many ADD adults tend to concentrate only on negative feedback and tend to feel unnecessarily insecure about their jobs. For example, Tom, a graduate school director of development, says he "used to feel like an axe was going to come down on me, but not accurately. I've done a superb job for my school, but I didn't feel like it."

Professional baseball player Scott Eyre, now a relief pitcher for the San Francisco Giants, used to ruminate over things he'd done wrong during games. "If I gave up a few runs, I'd get lost," he says. He used to walk home in his cleats after baseball games in high school because he was so tied up in the mistakes he'd made on the field and couldn't put them behind him. His failure even to change into normal shoes shows that he was, at least in his mind, still on the field, continuing to replay the game. He says that now, his wife and kids help him get over whatever happens during the game. "Nowa-

continued . . .

days, it doesn't matter, and I can put my frustration behind me. Now I see my two boys, and it doesn't matter what I did on the field."

Adults with ADD often have to work hard at recognizing their talents without allowing their weaknesses to engulf them and to color their entire self-image. ADD coach Jennifer Koretsky works with her clients to help them see their strengths and to combat their tendency to dwell on problems or mistakes. "Even if people are good at something, they're so bogged down by the things they're not good at," she says. "A lot of what we do in coaching is being able to acknowledge strengths and be thankful for them." Koretsky thinks the childhood of ADD adults primes them to concentrate on the negative. "If you're a problem in the school system when you're growing up, people tell you you're not listening. Even if you're fine in school, your room may be messy or you may have problems with friends. People around you give you a lot of feedback you don't want. You don't know why you can't keep your room clean. After hearing it long enough, people beat themselves up and the negative takes over."

If you have difficulty seeing your strengths or tend to dwell on the negative, you may want to enlist a trusted friend or work partner to remind you of what you do well. If the problem gets in the way of your work or happiness, psychotherapy may be useful to you.

■ To Tell or Not to Tell

The decision whether or not to tell your employer you have ADD is a complicated and personal one. There is no one right answer or correct way to do it. The adults interviewed for this book had a variety of experiences when they told their employers about having ADD, and the heterogeneity of their experiences points to the fact that the results of coming out of the proverbial ADD closet are as varied as the millions of workplaces and bosses in the workplace. More specific legal details about how to approach your employer to ask for accommodations under the federal Americans with Disabilities Act (ADA) are discussed in Chapter 11.

ADD and business coach Bonnie Mincu says that telling your employer you have ADD can be "a sticky issue, and it can backfire." She suggests that the first line of attack is "to tell your manager that 'I function best when _____' and to ask the employer to modify the environment without necessarily mentioning ADD at first. There's no saying how the manager will react, and it could hurt your career." She recommends mentioning that you have ADD only if you need extra time on a standardized test. Remember that during the hiring process, employers cannot by law ask whether you have a disability, so you are not legally compelled to mention that you have ADD when being considered for a job.

"There's still a lot of stigma," Mincu says. "It's getting a lot better, but [ADD] still means there's something wrong with you." Mincu suggests that if employees receive a warning about bad time management and if they are also working with a coach, they then tell the manager they've hired a "time management coach" without mentioning ADD. "Management likes to think someone is taking care of it," she says.

ADD coach Jennifer Koretsky encourages people to "advocate for themselves and be honest. Not everyone is comfortable saying they have ADD. No matter who the boss is, you can say 'I have a lot of trouble with invoices, but I'm good at presentations. Can we work it out? This assistant can help me with invoices, and I can do a good presentation.'"

Koretsky thinks it's positive if her clients want to tell their bosses explicitly that they have ADD. She recommends that they specifically tell the boss "why you need help and where you need it." She also says it's critical to include how these changes or accommodations will help the boss and what's in it for them. That means explaining how the worker will be more productive if the boss changes the way the employee works. Koretsky admits that "there is still a stigma attached to ADD, though I don't understand why it's a 'disability.'"

Let's look at a few cases of adults who shared their ADD diagnosis with their employers and how it worked for them.

Caroline, a computer instructor, decided to tell her boss that she has ADD because "my boss sat in on my first class as an instructor, and it was horrible, and I said I'd do better." Caroline believes that her organization is sensitive to lawsuits, and once they knew she had ADD, they gave her more time to put her classes together. "I don't think it's had a negative effect," she says. "It's helped."

Stacey, the physical education teacher, will bring up her ADD when it has to do with the children she works with at school. "I'll talk about it openly and joke about it," she says. "But I was very sensitive about it at first." Then she started bringing toys for people to play with during long, dull meetings. "It turned out over time that a lot of people identify with having ADD but don't talk about it," she says. "I'm light about it and just say, 'there goes my ADD.'" For Stacey, using a humorous approach allowed her co-workers to connect with her and to experience how her ADD could make their worklives more fun.

Not all workers with ADD feel that accommodations are helpful for them. Rachel, a psychiatrist, and Caitlin, a lawyer, both feel that they couldn't ask for accommodations because their work is too complex and independent. "Either I can do my job or not," Caitlin explains. "There's no reasonable accommodation to give me."

Sometimes, ADD adults, who often tend to be honest and impulsive, will spill the beans about having ADD and regret it later. For example, Zoe, a Manhattan sales executive, told her boss about having ADD, but now admits, "I'm sorry that I did. I'm very open and up-front. As long as I'm telling the truth, I think it's good. I wanted my boss to know my pitfalls and advise me, but I'm sorry now because his actions were tainted by it. He hasn't asked me to do certain things [after I told him] because he felt I didn't have time."

Zoe produced a log of how she spent every minute of the day and showed it to her boss "so he could find patterns and help me," she explains. She wanted to figure out why it took her so long to do her work and find ways to be more time-efficient, but "all I learned was that I work a lot and that it takes me more time than most people when I'm given new projects to tackle and that it takes me longer to get my arms around it. I'm more detailed in my delivery—the whole perfectionism thing, so my boss didn't find anything I could change."

Zoe says her boss's first reaction to her disclosure that she has ADD was that "he thinks it's bull. He's not informed about what it is. He doesn't believe in the concept of ADD. He says, 'you're just disorganized, you don't manage time well.'"

Zoe has also told other people at work about having ADD, but "it doesn't get a big reaction from people." If she loses her train of thought in a client meeting or if she forgets something midstream during a presentation, she'll tell people she has ADD. "It doesn't elicit a big response," she says. "I say it in a nonchalant way—not in an I-have-this-disease way."

ADD coach Becca Gross advises her clients to be wary of disclosing that they have ADD to their managers. "Think it through and consider all the pros and cons beforehand," she suggests. "Talking about your ADD can happen impulsively, so think about which accommodations are feasible and necessary and ask yourself whether it can happen in that organization and how receptive management will be." After asking themselves these questions, her clients sometimes conclude that their workplace is the wrong environment for them and decide to change jobs or careers rather than pursuing accommodations in their current job.

Gross suggests that if clients decide to approach their managers, they should mention specific issues such as that they work better in quiet areas or need their responsibilities to be more clearly defined. Because these accommodations are not always specifically related to ADD, it's not always necessary to mention that you have this condition.

Gross's advice comes from her personal experience working at a subsidiary of an international financial services company in the Netherlands—a country that arguably has even more generous employment laws than the United States does. Gross went through the process of asking for accommodations and making concrete suggestions that she thought would better her work in the information technology (IT) department at this financial services company. Her employer responded by saying that, despite Gross's requests to do so, Gross couldn't work in a private office or get a laptop because the employer would then have to provide these accommodations to everyone else as well. Gross had documentation from her doctor about her ADD, and she also hired a lawyer. In the end, she received severance pay and was let go. "Employers aren't interested in your productivity," she says. "They're interested in you're being like everyone else."

In many cases, workers are able to modify their jobs without mentioning their ADD. Lawyer Patricia Latham of Latham & Latham in Washington, D.C., has seen that often ADD adults are not successful at getting accommodations when they mention their disorder. She suggests that ADD adults consider using strategies to obtain informal accommodations without necessarily mentioning that they have ADD. "Say 'I'm more effective if I do this,'" she advises, "and sometimes, employers will work with you to provide what you need." For more information about asking for accommodations and finding out if you should pursue legal channels under the Americans with Disabilities Act (ADA), see Chapter 11.

Wilma Fellman, a career and life-planning counselor, works with many ADD adults who think they have to change careers and "throw out the baby with the bath water," when in fact, a little bit of modification will enable them to keep their jobs.

For example, Fellman helped salvage the job of a female emergency-room physician with ADD who worked at a major city hospital and who was in danger of getting fired. When she came to Fellman, this client thought she had to stop practicing medicine because she had poor time-management skills and simply couldn't keep up with the breakneck pace of her patient appointments. "Over the course of six months, we worked on defining where the process of day-to-day life was breaking down for her, and we learned some things from that exercise," Fellman says. "The client was unable to guess or differentiate between five and twenty-five minutes in her mind." The physician purchased the WatchMinder (see Chapter 2 for more information about this device) to teach her brain to recognize fifteen-minute intervals. Every fifteen minutes, she would program it to vibrate. "The doctor began to estimate more clearly what was around a fifteen-minute interval. We worked on programming the watch to give her a five-minute warning for being out of appointment, so she could gracefully be out of room and write a case note. There were no clocks in the nurses' station or where the attending physicians were, so she brought in cheap clocks and put them on the wall," Fellman explains.

"Slowly, it began to work for her," Fellman recalls. "A combination of things saved her job. The watch was a definite plus, as was identifying that time management was a problem for her." To lessen her stress, the client also reduced her workload to thirty hours per week. "When ADD people are stressed, they can't think anymore—a wall goes down," Fellman says.

■ The Human Resources Point of View

I conducted a number of interviews with human resources professionals and organizational consultants about their familiarity with ADD concerns. Although their policies varied, most were aware of the Americans with Disabilities Act (ADA) and stated that they would work with ADD employees who requested accommodations.

"I would like the employee to be direct about it," said a human resources manager at a large brokerage firm in the New York City area. "Say that you were diagnosed with ADD and these are the things I need. The more direct and honest you are, the better."

Another human resources manager at a financial-services firm in Boston said, "I would want [ADD adults] to disclose [their ADD] to determine reasonable accommodations for their case. If they don't disclose their ADD, they may not get the best accommodations. For example, if someone says they have difficulty focusing, it could mean many things, such as that they're too social. We need to know specifically their issues in the workplace and what accommodations they need."

It's important to note that the human resources professionals I spoke with had not had any direct experience working to provide an ADD employee with accommodations because no one had ever come forward in their organizations to let the HR department know he or she had ADD. Therefore, the HR professionals wanted to know more about the condition but were at this time largely uninformed about it. Even some mental-health professionals I spoke with had no idea of how prevalent ADD is in adulthood. It's interesting that the

HR professionals and organizational consultants I spoke with greatly overestimated the number of adults in the United States with ADD, which is estimated to be about 4 percent.[2] This implies that they think ADD is a widespread workplace issue, even if they've had no direct experience in dealing with it.

Human resources professionals also varied in whether they felt that having ADD could be an asset. One human resources manager in a financial-services firm thought that ADD would be an all-around disadvantage, while another HR manager in a large brokerage firm believed that ADD would be an advantage and believed (without supporting evidence) that many of the brokers in her firm have it. "Yes, ADD is an advantage because of the type of business we're in," she said. "The brokers are required to multitask. They're on the phone with two or more people at a time. It's not a structured, quiet environment. But ADD wouldn't work on the accounting or compliance side. It would work for something sales-related and high-pitched."

At this time, many human resources professionals and organizational consultants don't know that much about ADD, but they seem eager to learn. Many ask me interested questions and even seem convinced that many of their employees have ADD, even if they haven't identified themselves. In the coming years, as more and more adults acknowledge having ADD, human resources managers should develop a more informed, nuanced view of what it means to work with ADD.

---

[2] Murphy, K. R., & Barkley, R. A. (1996). Prevalence of *DSM-IV* symptoms of ADHD in adult licensed drivers. *Journal of Attention Disorders, 1,* 147–162.

• ◉ • CHAPTER HIGHLIGHTS • ◉ •

- The ideal boss allows the ADD adult to accomplish the job in his or her own way while providing guidance when needed. The best managers for ADD adults are flexible enough to allow employees to get their work done yet provide the requisite structure to be sure they stay on track.

- ADD employees don't tend to follow textbook methods of accomplishing their work. Managers who concentrate on the "right" way of doing things may find their ADD employees wanting. However, if the managers instead concentrate on results, they may value their ADD employees more and realize that they're getting what they need from their employees.

- In evaluating their relationships with their managers, it may be helpful for ADD adults to keep in mind that they often tend to concentrate only on negative feedback and to feel unnecessarily insecure about their jobs. It may help to consult a trusted colleague or friend about whether your perceptions are accurate.

- Deciding whether or not to tell your employer you have ADD is complex and depends on many factors. Be sure to consult with a lawyer or other qualified professional before specifically mentioning your ADD to your employer.

- Coaches and lawyers suggest that you can sometimes get the accommodations you need without specifically mentioning that you have ADD. If you do ask for accommodations, be sure to stress how they will benefit your employer.

- For more information about how to pursue legal channels to get accommodations at work, see Chapter 11.

■ Keep in mind that as of today, many human resources professionals may not understand ADD in adults or how it can be an asset in the workplace. They have not generally had the experience of working with an ADD employee who disclosed having ADD or requested special accommodations as a result of this condition.

PART 3

Getting Help

10

Working with ADD Coaches and Professional Organizers

> *"Coaching is an alchemical relationship—together with the client, coaches can make gold."*
>
> —LINDA ANDERSON, ADD COACH

What Is ADD Coaching?

The best athletic coach is someone who can give you skills and strategies to use on the playing field because he or she has played the game. ADD coaches are similar to athletic coaches. They work with ADD adults by helping them structure their work and achieve their goals in the context of understanding the very real struggles that adults with ADD face. Many coaches have ADD themselves or live with a spouse, partner, or child who does. They've studied how to live with ADD, read about the disorder, and offer help to others in a structured way. In some ways, they're not that different from good friends, except that they have enhanced knowledge about ADD and have seen what has worked well for other people with this condition. This chapter looks at what ADD coaches and professional organizers do and explains how you should go about looking for one that suits you and your needs.

▨ What You Should Know Before Hiring a Coach

Some coaches have social work or business degrees, but most do not. While there are many general life coaching institutes in the United States, specialized ADD coaches are trained primarily by taking phone classes (or "teleclasses") at two main ADD coaching institutes—the ADD Coach Academy in upstate New York and the Optimal Functioning Institute, which is a virtual organization based on the World Wide Web. There are various gradations of general coaches, including the top level of master certified coach (or MCC), but it is important to remember that these distinctions reflect the coaches' progression through the coaching institutes—and are not necessarily indicative of the coaches' worth or usefulness.

Coaches are not generally associated with universities, and they are not regulated by local, state, or federal agencies, such as medical doctors are. Therefore, it's best to think of coaching as a private arrangement in which the saying *caveat emptor,* or "buyer beware," applies. Many adults with ADD have found coaching very helpful, but at this time, there are no independent standards (outside those of the coaching institutes) to which every coach must adhere.

You should also be aware of when you need other types of assistance or need to supplement coaching with therapy or medication. Jeffrey P. Kahn, M.D., a New York City–area psychiatrist and president of WorkPysch Associates, an executive and corporate mental-health consulting firm, believes that sometimes coaching can prevent people from getting the deeper psychological help they need. "Coaches are psychological enablers," Dr. Kahn says. "In coaching, conflicts are not explored and relationships are not improved. Coaching provides a shoulder to cry on, which is not a bad thing, except to the extent that it prevents people from getting more effective help."

Dr. Kahn finds that many people with ADD also have anxiety and depressive disorders and that their ADD symptoms improve when they are treated through therapy and medication. "Often if a person's depression improves, their distractibility also improves," he says. People often come to him with self-diagnosed ADD. "Not uncommonly," he says, "there are also personality issues as well as anxiety or depressive disorder or both." Dr. Kahn advocates a treatment plan that focuses not only on ADD, but also on these co-occurring problems. Looking only at ADD is, in his words, "a surface view." Therefore, as you read about coaching, realize that you may need other types of help in addition to or instead of coaching. If you are at all in doubt of what kinds of help you need, consult a psychologist or medical doctor trained in mental health.

■ What Happens in Coaching

Coaching is a personalized process that enables you to work with someone you trust to achieve your desired goals. Coaches work with their clients to figure out how they work best and to provide accountability and support as the client progresses toward goals. Linda Anderson, an ADD coach based in Pennsylvania, describes coaching as a two-way dialogue that uses the energy between the client and coach to produce answers. "Solutions come out of the unique relationship with the client—you can brainstorm together," she says.

What Linda Anderson calls the "alchemical relationship" between client and coach forms the core of the process. Warren Simonoff, an ADD coach in Arizona, says that "the chemistry has to be right on both sides. A big piece of coaching is co-engineering solutions together." The coaching relationship is not like the typical expert-client relationship epitomized by the traditional doctor-patient interaction. Says Simonoff, "Coaches are not like consultants who say 'Do "ABC" and get back to me.'"

Eve, an architect and fashion designer who used a coach, advises ADD adults that in coaching, "YOU have to be in the driver's seat. If I were designing clothes, I would make them to fit you. If your coach is that attentive to your needs, then it will work for you," she says. "You have to give structure to coaching—don't get diverted from what you want to accomplish."

Jennifer Koretsky, an ADD coach in New York City, describes the coaching process as involving some experimenting. "We come up with strategies," she says. "If a client is really good at experimenting, we can figure out what works well quickly." She works to maximize clients' strengths, some of which they may not even recognize. "Even if they do acknowledge their strengths, they may be so bogged down by what they're not good at," she says. Coaching helps remedy clients' misapprehensions about their own talents and figure out how to put these talents to profitable use.

Coaching is a personalized process, so what it involves and how long it takes depend on the client. There is no established blueprint to guide you through the process. However, some challenges are common to most ADD coaching clients. Bonnie Mincu, a New York City–based business coach specializing in ADD adults, says that almost all her clients find it hard to get started on tasks. "The ADD roadblock is inexplicable to other people and coaches," she says. "They'd think the person was sabotaging himself." Mincu works with her clients to overcome their inertia for boring tasks by taking baby steps—a strategy she says works well across the board. How long the person works on these steps depends on the individual client. Mincu worked with a woman who was three years behind in her taxes and began by asking her to arrange the paper into piles.

She then worked with the client to write down all the necessary steps to complete her taxes and when to do them and supported her through the process.

Sometimes coaching involves homework. Coach Bonnie Mincu suggests people carry out actions toward reaching their goals by using what they're good at to accomplish what they're not good at. Mincu used to work as an organizational consultant and noticed that non-ADD executives often can't think out of the proverbial box, but she realized that many ADD adults can. She uses this characteristic ADD creativity to help people achieve their goals. For example, Mincu recently worked with a specialized consultant who was bored in his job and was casting about for a new entrepreneurial venture. He enjoyed helping people with home renovations, and he was adept at recommending the right workers and contractors for their specific problems. Through coaching with Mincu, he launched a home-improvement business as a unique kind of service that provided people with solutions to their home-maintenance problems. The client found that this new business took advantage of all his strengths.

Caroline, a computer instructor in the New Orleans area, used a coach while she was looking for a new job. She had worked as a paralegal and secretary for years, but she found that her job didn't draw on her strengths. The work was extremely frustrating and stressful, and she couldn't keep up with the detailed demands of co-workers who expected her to jump right into her tasks without explicitly spelling out what they wanted from her. With a career counselor, she determined that she would take the leap into computers—an area that had always interested her. During her stressful career transition, Caroline used a coach, which "helped me unbelievably," she says. "The coach told me how smart I was and made me feel confident. She gave me a different viewpoint when I was afraid to send my résumé out—she told me to just send it out and see what happened." Caroline says the coaching she received helped relieve some of her anxiety and educated her about ADD.

Caroline was eventually hired as a computer instructor and has become very effective in her work. She teaches people from the community who aren't comfortable with technology how to use basic computer software, and her awareness of her strengths allows her to use them on the job. "I know there's a lot of ways to get across the information," she says, "so I always tell my students to let me know the best way for them." She makes jokes and creates useful analogies to drive home concepts with her classes. "I compare folders on the computer to measuring cups—one nested inside the other," she says. Her creative methods of imparting information have helped make Caroline a popular teacher, and she has flourished in her new career, with the help of a supportive coach along the way.

■ The Nitty-Gritty of How Coaches Work

Each coaching relationship differs depending on the coach's style and background and what the client is looking to accomplish. However, the structure of the coaching process is fairly uniform. Coaches generally speak by phone with their clients three or four times per month. Some coaches offer in-person appointments, but the vast majority speak with their clients over the phone. This means that theoretically you can choose to work with any coach across the country. (See the section on how to choose a coach, below.)

Coaching sessions generally range in length from thirty to ninety minutes; the typical session lasts one hour. Between appointments, some coaches check in with clients by phone or e-mail. Coach Linda Anderson jots down challenges and resources that come up during sessions and then e-mails them to her clients within one day of their sessions. Anderson says this kind of follow-up is helpful to her clients because it reminds them of what they covered and shows them the map they've delineated to achieve their goals.

One coach mentioned that a man in the Coast Guard had recently asked her about e-mail coaching, which can be a possible route for people who like the medium or who can't get to a phone on a regular basis. Bonnie Mincu is beginning to test the waters for e-mail coaching, and this could be the wave of the future, although today, it's not the typically used medium.

How Is Coaching Different from Psychotherapy?

Coaching offers support, but it is not psychotherapy and isn't meant to take its place. According to ADD coach Linda Anderson, "Psychotherapy looks at why, but coaches don't go into that. Coaching goes into how, what, when." In other words, coaching tends to concentrate on developing practical solutions without necessarily investigating how the problems developed, while psychotherapy looks at the origin of problems and works to develop an awareness of clients' problem-solving styles.

Many adults choose to use both psychotherapy and ADD coaching to better their work and personal lives, and each process deals with different aspects of adult ADD life. Adults who have used the services of both coaches and psychotherapists tend to find coaching more directive. For example, Lois, an artist, grew up with a learning disability and undiagnosed ADD. She was the classic little girl daydreaming in the back of the classroom, and she had trouble reading and comprehending what went on in school. Her failure to understand what she read had a long-term impact on how she felt about herself, and she went to psychotherapy to understand herself and to address her feelings of inadequacy. She also used the services of an

ADD coach, a process that she found more action-oriented. Unlike psychotherapy, "Coaching didn't focus on me," she says, "but instead on what I wanted to do and how I wanted to do it." She worked with her coach to break things down into manageable steps, which helped her deal with the bombardment of creative ideas that come into her mind.

Rachel, a psychiatrist with ADD, found that her psychologist couldn't help her structure her life, so she turned to a coach. "Coaching helped me think through the process of how to do things in minute detail," she reports. Rachel had used informal coaches for years before the coaching industry even got off the ground. For example, when she was a medical intern, she hired her roommate to help her organize her files and her schedule. "Non-ADD people have an internal sense of how to organize their lives and structure things," she says. "If you don't know this as an adult, there's nowhere to get it. The coach is the only one whose job it is to help you organize yourself."

How to Choose a Coach

Bonnie Mincu, the business and ADD coach in New York City, suggests speaking to a few coaches—generally about three—before you select the person who's best for you. "Ask the credentials of the coach—including how long they've been a coach and who've they coached," she suggests. "See what it's like to talk to them and what your rapport with them is like." Mincu advises entrepreneurs to ask if the coach has worked with entrepreneurs before and if the coach understands the specific pressures and challenges involved in starting a business.

Linda Anderson suggests that would-be coaching clients take the time to find out how the potential coach listens to them as they talk.

"Listen to what the coach sounds like," she advises, "and ask your-self 'Can I work with him or her?'" She also thinks it's useful for clients to find out if the coach is comfortable working on what the clients want to achieve. Anderson usually spends fifteen to thirty minutes talking to someone without a fee before the person decides whether she will be his or her coach.

A great number of ADD coaches have ADD themselves. Coaches differ on whether ADD coaches need to have the condition to be effective. Many ADD adults have been helped by coaches who don't have ADD. Coach Becca Gross says her clients value her insight into their experience, but having ADD doesn't necessarily make that part happen.

Coaches generally agree that the most basic elements of being a good ADD coach are understanding how the adult ADD brain works and understanding how the inner workings of the ADD mind manifest themselves in daily life. Coach Jennifer Koretsky says it's vital that coaches realize that "if the client doesn't show up, that doesn't equal lack of motivation." She believes that a coach with ADD can understand what it's like to be in the place where client is and what it takes to move beyond it. "ADD adults have lived most of their lives without others giving them understanding, so the abil-ity of the coach to empathize is important," she says.

You can find a list of coaches across the country on the website of the Attention Deficit Disorder Association (ADDA) at www.add.org, or from ADD Consults at www.addconsults.com. On the ADD Con-sults website, you can find out details about each coach's training and philosophy and contact coaches.

■ Paying for Coaching

Coaching is expensive by most workers' standards—especially if you are in between jobs—and the high price is generally what gets in the way of ADD adults getting coached. Monthly fees for three or four sessions range from $300 to $600, and the typical fee is about $100 to $125 per hour. Coaches who work with executives tend to charge more, and very experienced coaches charge $250 to $500 per hour. Some beginning coaches offer much lower rates, even down to about $40 per hour.

Health insurance plans generally do not cover the cost of coaching, although some coaches advise you to look into your flexible spending accounts to see if you can use that pre-tax money for coaching. If you are using coaching for a business problem, you may be able to write some of the expense off on your taxes; coaches suggest speaking to your accountant about this deduction.

What if you feel that you can't afford coaching but would like to try it? There are a few things you can do. First, although coaches often won't mention this up front, many have so-called sliding scales. This means they may be willing to negotiate a lower fee, particularly if they feel you are very motivated to achieve your goals. Second, many coaches offer a certain number of scholarships for clients who aren't able to pay. On the ADD Consults website (www. addconsults.com), some of the coaches specifically mention that they provide scholarships.

Finally, many coaches offer in-person groups or "teleclasses" for a lot less money than individual coaching. These services also offer you the opportunity to connect with other ADD adults. A typical group could cost about $150 for four ninety-minute sessions, which breaks down to $25 per hour.

Teleclasses cost about $20 to $30 for a session that lasts sixty to ninety minutes. A typical teleclass involves dialing into a bridge number (which is not toll-free) and being connected to a group of about fifteen to thirty other people. The first part of the session may involve a lecture from a coach about an aspect of ADD such as how to initiate projects. Coaches leading the session can mute out everyone's else sounds so listeners aren't distracted by unwanted noise during the lecture. The lecture is followed by a discussion session. There may also be written backup to the session. Coach Bonnie Mincu, for example, has arranged a system by which callers can dial into a number to listen to the class for up to a week later, and she also e-mails participants a detailed set of notes so they don't have to wear out their hands taking notes during the lecture.

It's also important to note that coaching, particularly for entrepreneurs, may wind up paying off in increased revenues that could cover the cost of coaching. Lois, an artist, says she made three times as much money when she was receiving coaching than when she stopped using a coach.

Career Counselors

Career counselors can help you sort out your aptitudes and interests and work with you in a collaborative way to determine your career path. Career planning may be particularly important for adults with ADD because they have so many interests and passions and have a difficult time limiting their focus and concentrating on the most productive option. As actress and filmmaker Winona says, "My therapist kept saying that people with ADD can imagine themselves anywhere, and it's true." ADD adults also may need help in developing a step-by-step strategy to work through the sometimes-overwhelming process of looking for a new job or planning a career change.

Wilma Fellman, a career and life planning counselor who has worked with and written about the career planning process for ADD adults, suggests that people go about finding a career counselor "in the same way they find a therapist. It is a match of need, background, and personality fit." She advises potential clients to contact more than one counselor in their area to find out their background and how often they've worked with someone with disabilities. The average career counseling process lasts about ten sessions, and Fellman says you should continue in the process, "as long as you're constantly gaining more information and the counselor is helping you put it together."

The average career counseling session lasts an hour and costs about $80, though hourly rates for private counseling range from $60 to $120. Public service agencies have sliding scales down to $5 hour if their funding comes from other sources. "There are wonderful ways to go for no cost," Fellman says. "All universities have career counseling centers, as do community colleges. A person who's a resident of the county can get free career counseling." To find a career counselor or psychologist to help you with career transitions, go to www.addconsults.com or www.addresources.org. For more information about how ADD adults have used career counseling to find a career that is the right fit for them, see Chapter 6.

■ Professional Organizers

While ADD coaches help you conceptually understand how to tackle your goals, organizers provide hands-on support with instituting physical systems that keep you on track. They give you a game plan for getting your physical space in order and prioritizing how you will begin to attack the clutter.

New York City organizer Sondra Schiff works to "optimize clients' space, time, and systems." She first assesses her clients' home or work environments with an eye toward what works for them and their goals. "I want to see what they want to experience

Writing Coaches

Though it's not (yet) an established industry, you can find a writing coach who has an awareness of how ADD adults tend to write and how they can improve their written products. Don Tapken, based in Albany, New York, is ABD (all-but-dissertation) in English literature, and he has helped clients with ADD with their work-related writing projects and graduate school papers. Writing projects tend to present difficulties for many ADD adults, who dislike the attention to detail and the tedious revision inherent in the process.

Tapken has an understanding of the particular grammatical and structural snafus that often trip up people with ADD. "They have a tendency to come up with run-on sentences and use a dash," he explains. "This enables them to change thoughts in the middle of the sentence and use a dash to legitimize it." He also finds that ADD writers tend to have sudden shifts of tone, such as from formal writing to an informal joke, without preparing their readers for what's going to come next. He works to find writers' good ideas, which are often buried in their writing, and to highlight them.

Tapken works with his clients in a supportive way, offering critiques rather than criticisms and throwing out alternatives rather than mandates. "When I put my clients' ideas into workable prose," he says, "they are flabbergasted at how good it sounds. They then realize their ideas are meaningful—the problem isn't the quality of the ideas, but their expression." Tapken currently charges about $25 per hour.

emotionally and physically in their space or system," she says. "They usually want peace and quiet—something like the feeling that they experience in the yoga studio."

Being organized doesn't mean your house looks like a spread in *Architectural Digest,* according to longtime New York organizer Donna Goldberg. "Organization is about being able to put your hands on the most important things when you need to get to them, not about being neat and orderly," says Goldberg. "You don't want to fix what isn't broken even if it looks like chaos to the outside world. It's only a problem when you don't have a system so you can't retrieve something and can't meet deadlines."

Veteran professional organizer Denslow Brown says that in working with ADD clients, "You're looking for a really different solution and are willing to do more eccentric things that don't look normal in general." Brown, who has also been trained as an ADD coach, works with the strengths and preferential styles of her clients. One of her clients had a lot of physical energy and complained that her office was so disorganized that she could only spend a short time there before having to leave. When Brown suggested moving files the client needed to a more convenient drawer, the client looked at Brown with a confused expression. "The client liked to get out of her chair," Brown says. "We rearranged her office to allow her to jump up and down all the time. She can now work there all the time." Although this solution may have seemed odd to the non-ADD adult, it was right for this client.

Professional organizer Laura Lakin sometimes works with clients who have unrealistic expectations, which she calls the "magic wand syndrome, but I don't have one." They want all the clutter to disappear immediately, but it generally takes some time for workable systems to be put into place. The average time with which she works with a client is about four or five sessions, but she has worked with some clients for much longer. "You cannot snap your fingers and become an ordinary worker," she says about ADD adults, noting that ADD workers have special skills that set them apart but that they can't expect to get organized in a flash.

As with coaching, the process of using a professional organizer varies by client and is geared to the client's stated goals. Some clients use professional organizers just to prime the pump and get the system started, while others want a more hands-on service to get their physical space in order because they haven't been successful doing it on their own in the past. "Sometimes just being with my clients helps them focus," says Schiff. "They can then create dedicated time for organizing."

Each client finds a different kind of physical space that is conducive to focus and concentration. "Sometimes I quiet down the client's environment, and sometimes I stimulate it," Schiff says. For example, she may advise the client to lower the volume on the television but not turn it off because a certain amount of ambient sound keeps him or her focused. Schiff has stimulated work environments by bringing more color into the room for someone feeling deadened by the space or by bringing color into the client's filing system. Atlanta-based organizer Poppy Cantrell often starts with people's private spaces. "The bed and bath nourish you— they're your retreat. They should look serene visually, not chaotic. Once that area is taken care of, it inspires them to go into more public areas."

Schiff also works with her clients to slow down their impulse to buy new things because many ADD adults are compulsive acquisitors of trinkets. What people collect is different for different people; Schiff mentions that she's seen overwhelming collections of ribbons, collectibles, and wrapping paper. "Culling is difficult," she says, "so first I help them identify what's a treasure by getting their stuff together. It's easier to make a decision, for example, if you see all your scarves together."

Professional organizer Laura Lakin suggests that ADD adults concentrate on one area that is a priority for them and start there. "The best strategy is to ask the client where would you like to begin and what is driving you the most crazy. They frequently point to the dining room table. It's best to focus on one area first because ADD clients may get panicked by looking around the whole room." Lakin works intensively in the area that the person thinks needs improvement first. She also finds that some ADD clients tend not to have equipment such as pencil cups on their desks, and it's a "small but good victory" to introduce such organizing tools into the client's environment.

Organizing can focus on both home and work environments. Poppy Cantrell works to institute systems that help entire families. She often starts working with the mother of the family, but her changes have an organizing effect on the entire family. "I draw a road map that labels where things are and stick it up on the closet door," she explains. "There's a guide for when the system disintegrates. It's helpful when kids can put things away and don't just dump them because they don't know where they go. It teaches kids skills."

Donna Goldberg recently worked with an attorney to organize his work processes. She observed him take call after call during which clients would continually ask if he had followed up on small-picture details. Though the lawyer had many associates who worked for him, he didn't delegate these kinds of tasks. Although he had different forms to track things, he never used them for himself. He would scribble what he had to do on a legal pad and then frenetically rush to his next meeting. Goldberg created a tracking sheet on 11 by 17-inch paper to accommodate the lawyer's large, scrawling handwriting and to allow him to record four phone calls on each page. The sheet tracked the day of the call, the client's name, what action the lawyer needed to take, and how the information came to him—either from a meeting, e-mail, or snail mail. His secretary collected these sheets several times per day and used them to generate a to-do list. These sheets also became the basis for the lawyer's billing and streamlined his entire practice.

■ Working with a Professional Organizer

The duration, number of sessions, and cost of working with an organizer vary widely. Although two sessions might be sufficient to organize a home office, many ADD clients find it difficult to sustain a new system and call their organizer back for what Sondra Schiff refers to as "fine-tuning."

Seasoned organizers currently run about $80 up to $200 per hour, while new organizers charge about $50 per hour. Some organizers also offer classes at local community centers that cost about $150 for a four-week class. If you are working to organize an office or home office, you can, based on your accountant's advice, list organizing fees as business expenses if you itemize your taxes.

Some organizers are also ADD coaches. Missouri-based Denslow Brown, who began working as an organizer around the time the field was coming together thirty years ago, also has been trained and works as a coach. She does coaching and organizing simultaneously and calls herself an "organizer/coach." Though most organizers work on-site, Brown also organizes people's desks long-distance by phone and has many clients in other areas of the country.

"If a client is sitting at a messy desk, I can talk them through organizing the desk. I have seen so many desks that I can imagine it," she says. "It's possible to be a voice in their ear and help them think through the decisions and choices they have. If they're physically doing it, they own it." Brown believes this type of organizing can be advantageous because the client is taking control of his or her own systems. "As an organizer, I would work to make a home beautiful, and I would leave proud of what I did, but I knew the person couldn't maintain the filing system or clean office. I would tell them I was happy to come back, but the system was peaking when I left."

■ How to Choose an Organizer

Veteran organizer Donna Goldberg suggests that people looking to hire an organizer ask professionals they're considering working with how long they've been in the field and the types of people and projects they've worked with. Organizer Sondra Schiff suggests interviewing prospective organizers to see if your chemistry mixes well and asking for references. She advises people not to buy into expensive packages but to have an initial session and not to shell out any money up front.

For more information about professional organizers, contact the National Study Group on Chronic Disorganization (www.NSGCD.org) and the National Association of Professional Organizers (NAPO) at www.napo.net. On the NSGCD website, you can e-mail the referral coordinator to find a professional organizer, and you can see the list of their graduates with different levels of training. On the NAPO website, you can enter your ZIP code and get a list of local organizers. You can also select organizers who have specific experience with ADD clients or with such tasks as paper, home offices, or writing.

• ● • CHAPTER HIGHLIGHTS • ● •

- ADD coaches offer structured support with an awareness of the way this condition complicates people's lives.

- While many adults with ADD feel that they have been greatly helped by ADD coaches, there is no legal regulation of the industry and no outside standards to which coaches must adhere. This means that the onus is on the person purchasing the coach's services to do his or her homework and find a good personal fit with a coach who will be of benefit to him or her.

- There is no blueprint to coaching; it's a personalized process. The duration of the coaching and the goals you set out to achieve are up to you.

- Most coaching takes place on the phone; the typical session lasts an hour and occurs three or four times per month. Some coaches use e-mail for follow-up notes and for contact between sessions.

- Coaching differs from psychotherapy in its intent; coaching concentrates on how you can achieve your goals and not specifically on understanding yourself as a person. Adults with ADD who have used both ADD coaches and psychotherapists report that each process is helpful for different purposes and that coaching tends to be more directive.

- Coaches suggest that you interview a few potential coaches— typically about three—to decide if you have a good rapport with the person and if the person will be able to work with you on what you want to accomplish.

- Coaching typically costs about $100 per hour. Some coaches offer "sliding scales" and will negotiate a lower fee for very motivated clients or offer scholarships. Less experienced coaches tend to offer lower fees. "Teleclasses," which involve lectures and group coaching on the phone, and groups are other, less expensive ways to receive coaching.

- Professional organizers can help you hands-on to streamline your physical and mental space. As with coaching, the process of organizing varies by client, and you should investigate a few organizers to find one with whom you work well.

11

Your Legal Rights

"One of the big problems I'm seeing is that a lot of people overestimate their rights under the ADA."

—PATRICIA LATHAM, J.D.

■ The Americans with Disabilities Act (ADA)

Under the federal Americans with Disabilities Act (ADA) of 1990, employers are required by law to provide "reasonable accommodation" for otherwise qualified employees and applicants with disabilities, unless these accommodations pose "undue hardship" to the employer. The Job Accommodation Network (on the Web at www. jan.wvu.edu) found that the majority of accommodations that employers have made for people with disabilities do not cause hardship to employers and cost under $500.

It is important to note that employees and job applicants are responsible for making their disabilities known to the employer to be able to request accommodations. Employers are not required to make accommodations if they aren't aware of the employee's need for them. The ADA covers employees of all state and local governments, educational organizations, and private employers that have fifteen or more employees. You can link to the entire text of the ADA and read related government publications on the "Employment" section of the website of Children and Adults with Attention-Deficit/Hyperactivity Disorder (CHADD) at www.chadd.org.

But how does the process of advocating for your rights under the ADA actually work, and can you make it work for you? This chapter provides an explanation of how to pursue your legal rights and will give you an idea of whether this will be a worthwhile avenue for you.

■ The First Step: Consulting a Lawyer

Before asking for accommodations, you should consult a lawyer who practices in the area of disabilities and employment law. If you cannot afford a lawyer, many free services can be of help. In addition, the Job Accommodation Network (on the Web at www.jan. wvu.edu or by phone at 1-800-ADA-WORK or 1-800-526-7234) offers a free consulting service that provides information about accommodations under the ADA.

Patricia Latham of Latham & Latham in Washington, D.C., a lawyer who has written extensively about ADD and the law, suggests that people who are interested in finding out about their rights under the ADA consult a lawyer who specializes in employment law: "Find a lawyer who's familiar with different rules and regulations and who's able to advise you if you meet the test and are disabled under the law, are qualified for your job, and whether the accommodations you're proposing are reasonable." If you live in a major metropolitan area, you can check with your local chapter of CHADD, ADDA, or the Learning Disabilities Association of America to find a lawyer who works in the disabilities area (see Helpful Resources at the end of the book for contact information for these organizations).

Latham urges people to be careful about seeking protection under the ADA. "One of the big problems I'm seeing is that a lot of people overestimate their rights under the ADA," she says. "It's a bigger problem than underestimating your rights." She suggests that if you believe you've been wronged in the workplace, it's a good idea to arrange a one-hour consult with a lawyer. Most lawyers charge about $200 for this consult, though some might do it for free.

"Do the consult with a lawyer before you start taking positions at work," Latham suggests. "Before you start pounding the table and demanding things, find out if you have a meritorious position." She advises people to consult a lawyer before they disclose that they have ADD or write a letter requesting accommodations.

"If you have ADD, it's not necessarily true that you have a disability under the law," she warns. "What you have to be able to show is that you're substantially limited in a major life activity compared to average people." Although many ADD adults have impaired functioning in some ways, they are, in Latham's words, "still functioning in major ways approximately as well as average people. If that's true, you would have difficulty establishing that you are disabled under the law," she says.

According to Latham, the only meritorious position under which you could pursue accommodations under the ADA is if your ADD causes you to be substantially limited in a major life activity compared to other people. The law also looks at your functioning with your medication, and because some adults with ADD function very well with medication, they're not considered disabled under the law.

Latham explains to her clients that 95 percent of cases relating to disabilities in employment law are won by employers. "The problem is that if you were substantially limited by ADD, you would be substantially impaired and wouldn't be able to do a lot of jobs." She suggests that people with ADD work to come up with their own compensation strategies to help them function at their best and that they collaborate with their employers to develop the best possible resolution that will benefit both the employer and the employee. People who don't have a strong legal position should politely ask their employers for accommodations, she advises.

▓ How to Ask for Accommodations

The ADA does not stipulate specific guidelines or forms that you should use to ask your employer for accommodations. If your employer has specific forms for requesting an accommodation, you should use them. If not, there is no specific format you must follow. The Job Accommodation Network, at www.jan.wvu.edu, offers a very useful template for writing a letter requesting accommodations from your employer. You can consult these guidelines and customize them for your purposes. According to the Job Accommodation Network, the major points of your letter should be as follows:

- State that you have a disability.

- State that you are requesting job accommodations under the ADA (or under the Rehabilitation Act of 1973, if you are employed by the federal government).

- Cite the specific job tasks that are causing problems for you.

- Offer your ideas about accommodations that will resolve these problems.

- Ask the employer to contribute ideas about accommodations to help you.

- Attach medical documentation that backs up your claim to have disabilities, if you have such paperwork.

• Ask your employer to respond to your requests within a reasonable time frame.

◼ What Kinds of Accommodations Can You Ask For?

The Job Accommodation Network (on the Web at www.jan.wvu.edu) offers a list of specific accommodations to resolve problems with reading, writing, math, organizational skills, and distractions in the physical work environment. Its website also gives examples of simple accommodations that have helped actual workers in a range of fields, including managerial, service, and industrial employees with ADD. These include very simple changes in the work environment or in work processes, such as the provision of oral instructions, purchasing color-coded files, and using white-noise machines to limit distractions. The cost of each accommodation is included. Some, such as shifting work hours and providing oral instructions, cost absolutely nothing, and others, such as purchasing an inexpensive daily calendar, involve minimal cost to the employer or to the employee.

Reading this list of accommodations before you compose a letter to your employer may give you ideas of job restructuring or of assistive technologies that will be appropriate for your situation. Before you send the letter to your employer, you may want to ask a lawyer or a trusted co-worker or friend who is knowledgeable about your employment situation to read it over to see if your requests are suitable and make sense. You want to be sure your letter is effective because it provides the opening of a dialogue between you and your employer—a conversation that you want to result in helpful changes that will be beneficial both to you and your employer. Your employer may be more willing to grant these accommodations if you provide evidence, based on the Job Accommodation Network's website, that such accommodations have yielded good results for similar employees in the past and that they can be made at little or no cost to employers.

What If You're Fired?

Even if you are fired from your job, don't make the mistake of thinking that the ADA necessarily offers restitution. According to attorney Patricia Latham, "You should still talk to a lawyer. Find out: Was I properly fired or improperly fired? You can still try to negotiate the best possible exit package."

Latham notes that having ADD doesn't protect you from being dismissed. "If your ADD causes you to make mistakes at work, your employer may be able to properly fire you. The ADA requires you to be qualified for the job. If you can't get to work on time, you won't be qualified for most jobs."

Again, it's best to take a considered approach to advocating for your rights under the ADA. A knowledgeable lawyer will enable you to find the best solution—one that may not involve your mentioning having ADD.

• ◉ • CHAPTER HIGHLIGHTS • ◉ •

- Under the federal Americans with Disabilities Act (ADA), you are required to make your disability known to your employer before requesting accommodations.

- Before requesting accommodations, consult a lawyer or contact a free service, such as the Job Accommodations Network (www.jan. wvu.edu, or 1-800-ADA-WORK), for guidance.

- You don't automatically have rights under the ADA. Be sure to consult a lawyer to see if you meet the legal criteria before assuming that having ADD definitely constitutes a disability under the ADA.

- If you decide, based on a lawyer's advice, to request specific accommodations, compose a letter identifying your disabilities and spelling out the specific accommodations you would like. Use your employer's forms if they are available, or write a letter following the template on the Job Accommodation Network website.

- Use the list of accommodations on the Job Accommodation Network website to get an idea of possible accommodations and how much they cost. These accommodations will allow you to write a letter based on what has worked for similar employees in the past and to assure your employer that these changes and devices work and aren't generally expensive.

- If you are fired, don't assume you are protected under the ADA. Consult with a lawyer to find out if you have a meritorious case and to get the best exit package.

Fulfilling the Promise of ADD at Work

While ADD poses real challenges to the millions of children and adults who have it, it's easy to see that people with this so-called disability also have incredible gifts. As Jennifer Stewart, an actress who has played Lady Liberty through her company Living Liberty, says, "[Having ADD] is the reason I like liberty. The real challenge is how do we change and improve on what we're given? How can I focus on the positive and create change? That's what liberty is about."

Increasing awareness about ADD offers those who have it the opportunity to build on their gifts and transform them into something greater and to offer novel solutions and ways of looking at the world. This book has attempted to present a full picture of adult ADD in an effort to understand its complications and to help those who have it thrive in today's work world.

As we've seen, ADD in adults bucks conventional wisdom and is not a death sentence or career killer. Instead, it is a nuanced condition that presents opportunities for enormous success at the same time it complicates that success. The scores of phenomenal adults interviewed for this book were able to reach their career goals by developing smart work skills, finding a workplace suited for them, and getting help from others if needed. This three-pronged approach allowed them to manage their ADD without letting it destroy what they had worked so hard for.

It is no exaggeration to say that I thoroughly enjoyed speaking to the adults whom I interviewed for this book. They were without fail open, honest, kind, and funny. They often didn't fully recognize their special gifts—even if they were top medical doctors, successful businesspeople, or brilliant artists. It is my great wish to help them understand how talented they are and how much energy and dynamism they have. When I tired in my research, a conversation with one of these adults always sparked my interest anew and compelled me to go on in my work. I hope the ideas and strategies in this book will help them, and others like them, see their unique talents and use them to their fullest advantage—and to that of the greater world.

Helpful Resources

Organizations and Websites

ADD Consults: On the Web at www.addconsults.com. On this site, "the first and only virtual online ADD clinic," you can find a coach or other professional, participate in teleclasses or online coaching, and ask a professional a question. The site also offers free online chat groups and relevant articles. There is also an online store with useful products, including organizational tools, fidget toys, and clothing for people who are attuned to the way fabrics feel.

Attention Deficit Disorder Association (ADDA): On the Web at www.add.org. ADDA is an information, networking, and advocacy group. On its website, you can find a list of coaches, psychologists, and other professionals and services, though these professionals are not endorsed by the ADDA. They also have support groups all over the country.

Address: ADDA
P.O. Box 543
Pottstown, PA 19464
Phone: (484) 945-2101
Fax: (610) 970-7520
E-mail: mail@add.org

Attention Deficit Disorder Resources (ADD Resources): On the Web at www.addresources.org. Its website has a directory of doctors, coaches, tutors, educational consultants, career counselors, and other service providers. The website also links to other ADD-related sites and contains articles and a bookstore.

Address: Attention Deficit Disorder Resources
223 Tacoma Avenue S, #100
Tacoma, WA 98402
Phone: (253) 759-5085 (Monday–Friday 11:30 A.M.–2:30 P.M.)

Children and Adults with Attention-Deficit/Hyperactivity Disorder (CHADD): On the Web at www.chadd.org. A nonprofit ADD organization with more than 20,000 members and 200 affiliates across the country, it provides information and advocacy and publishes *ATTENTION!* magazine. You can find educational articles, discussion groups, and local support groups on its website. They also run the National Resource Center on AD/HD.

Address: CHADD
8181 Professional Place, Suite 150
Landover, MD 20785
National Resource Center on AD/HD: (800) 233-4050
Business: (301) 306-7070

Job Accommodation Network: Call 1-800-ADA-WORK or visit its website at www.jan.wvu.edu for additional information regarding the ADA and reasonable accommodations. They provide a free information line about accommodations.

Latham & Latham: On the Web at www.lathamlaw.org. On this site, you can order videos and books by Peter S. Latham, J.D., and Patricia Horan Latham, J.D., attorneys in Washington, D.C. Their titles include revised editions of *ADD and the Law* and *Learning Disabilities and the Law,* published by JKL Communications.

Address: Latham & Latham
2700 Virginia Avenue NW, Suite 707
Washington, DC 20037
Phone: (202) 333-1713
Fax: (202) 333-1735
E-mail: Plath@lathamlaw.org

Landmark College: On the Web at www.landmark.edu. An accredited college specifically for students with ADD, dyslexia, and other learning disabilities, it also offers workshops and training for educators and administrators about helping students with learning issues.

Address: Landmark College
River Road South
Putney, VT 05346
Admissions: (802) 387-6718
All other inquiries: (802) 387-4767

Learning Disabilities Association of America: On the Web at www.ldanatl.org. This is the nation's largest nonprofit advocacy group for people with learning disabilities with more than 200 affiliates nationwide and in Puerto Rico and a membership of 40,000 people worldwide. Its website allows you to find articles, resources, research, and books of interest and to connect with local support groups.

Address: Learning Disabilities Association of America
4156 Library Road
Pittsburgh, PA 15234-1349
Phone: (412) 341-1515
Fax: (412) 344-0224

National Association of Professional Organizers: On the Web at www.napo.net. Its automated referral system allows you to find an organizer in your area with experience in specific areas, such as ADD, home offices, or paper management.

Address: National Association of Professional Organizers
4700 W. Lake Avenue
Glenview, IL 60025
Referral line: (847) 375-4746
Fax: (877) 734-8668
International and Canada fax: (732) 578-2636
E-mail: hq@napo.net

National Study Group on Chronic Disorganization: On the Web at www.nsgcd.org. You can find assistance from a professional organizer who has experience with chronic disorganization by e-mailing your name, address, and phone numbers (day/evening) and e-mail to cdreferral@nsgcd.org. They ask you to indicate your specific needs—home, home office, business or workplace, or student assistance.

Technological Tools

Bose Noise-Canceling Headphones: The Bose Quiet Comfort® acoustic noise-canceling headphones identify and reduce undesirable noise before it enters your ears, allowing more of the music, words, or silence you desire to reach you. The headphones have an ergonomic, lightweight design. The earphones cost about $199; visit www.bose.com for more information.

Magellan GPS Driving Software: These mapping software and portable global positioning systems facilitate driving. The Magellan GPS lets you know where you are at any given moment, your speed, and the distance and time until you reach your destination. The company also makes lightweight handheld devices equipped with mapping systems. Call 1 (800) 707-9971 or visit www.magellan gps.com for information and prices.

Dragon Naturally Speaking: These software programs allow you to work with your Windows program by only using your voice and without touching the keyboard, or by using a combination of voice, keyboard, and mouse. The program allows you to dictate an e-mail message to send out over the Internet and to read aloud numbers from a spreadsheet and enter them by voice into a database. The program also enables you to dictate at speeds up to 160 words per minute and saves transcription costs. Available at www.amazon.com and other websites.

Kurzweil 3000: This software for PC and Macintosh platforms speaks letters and words as you type and identifies spelling mistakes and incorrect words. You can have the program read back your writing to be sure it makes sense and to facilitate proofreading. The software, which has color and black-and-white versions, is available in various packages at different prices; the black-and-white software for individual use was around $1,000 at the time of publication, while the color software cost about $1,500. You also need to purchase an Epson scanner so you can scan your reading materials. For more information, call (800) 894-5374 or visit www.kurzweiledu.com.

WatchMinder: This digital watch uses a vibration system (you feel it but don't hear it, so it's private) and visual prompts to remind you to take your medication, check e-mail, go to work, go to your coach, pay bills, and about seventy other customizable commands. Call (800) 961-0023 or visit www.watchminder.com for more information.

Books

Barkley, Russell A. *Taking Charge of ADHD, Revised Edition.* Guilford Press: 2000.

———. *Attention-Deficit Hyperactivity Disorder: A Handbook for Diagnosis and Treatment,* Second Edition. Guilford Press: 1998.

Bolles, Richard Nelson. *What Color Is Your Parachute?: A Practical Manual for Job-Hunters and Career Changers.* Ten Speed Press, updated continuously.

Fellman, Wilma R. *Finding a Career That Works for You: A Step-by-Step Guide to Choosing a Career and Finding a Job.* Specialty Press, Incorporated: 2000.

Glovinsky, Cindy. *Making Peace with the Things in Your Life.* St. Martin's Press: 2002.

Hallowell, Edward M., and Ratey, John J. *Driven to Distraction: Recognizing and Coping with Attention Deficit Disorder from Childhood Through Adulthood.* Pantheon Books: 1994.

Kelly, Kate, and Ramundo, Peggy. *You Mean I'm Not Lazy, Stupid, or*

Crazy?! A Self-Help Book for Adults with Attention Deficit Disorder. Scribner: 1995.

Latham, Peter S., and Latham, Patricia H. *ADD and the Law, Second Edition.* JKL Communications: 1997.

Latham, Patricia H., Ratey, Nancy and Latham, Peter S. *Tales from the Work Place.* JKL Communications: 1997.

Nadeau, Kathleen G. *ADD in the Workplace.* Brunner/Mazel: 1997.

Quinn, Patricia Q., editor. *ADD and the College Student, Revised Edition.* Magination Press: 2001.

Solden, Sari. *Women with Attention Deficit Disorder.* Underwood Books: 1995.

Weiss, M., Hechtman, L. T. and Weiss, G. . *ADHD in Adulthood: A Guide to Current Theory, Diagnosis, and Treatment.* Johns Hopkins University Press: 1999.

Index

About the Author

Blythe Grossberg, Psy.D., is a career consultant with a doctoral degree in Organizational Psychology, who specializes in adult Attention Deficit Disorders. She has written for *Boston Magazine, The Radcliffe Quarterly,* and *Travel & Leisure,* and has worked for *The New Yorker.* She is a member of the national Attention Deficit Disorder Association (ADDA) and has conducted a two-year study on ADHD adults in the workplace. She lives and practices in New York City.